This book is dedicated
to my parents

Reviews from Mostly Non-Vegans

"I was invited to attend one of Hila's vegan food parties in January 2018 and wow the food was unlike anything I've ever sampled! I kept saying "I can't believe it's not cheese" about the cheese, and the other creations were very tasty and I felt very healthy (and full) afterwards. Totally recommended".

Sorcha Ress Chisholm

"Exceptional taste, sophisticated presentation and mindfully prepared. Simply amazing".

Katrina MacLachlan

"It's not only about the fantastic food but it's about the art and the passion of what Hila is designing on the plate".

Craciun Cati Loredana

"The first time I tried Hila's food I felt my pallet opened up. The food is just divine! I am an absolute fan now of her beautifully created food!"

Kerstin Sekimoto

"Hila is amazing at details! Her presentation of her food is always so pleasing to the eye. Taste is always amazing! I appreciate how she brings out the flavours of the vegetables and fruits and allows them to shine without using a lot of seasoning. If you are interested in incorporating more plant based foods or moving into veganism, but are concerned you will miss your favorite dishes, I assure you Hila will have a dish that will satisfy your cravings for comfort. Love all of her creations!"

Megumi Rubenstein

"Hila makes the most delicious and nutritious food!"

Lee Bruce

"Healthy, beautiful food! I highly recommend Zen Lady Tokyo!"

Kyoko Hashimoto

"The new generation of delicatessen. Thank you Hila".

David Brisson

"The food is absolutely amazing!!! The first time I heard about raw vegan and started loving it. Now I just need the same talent to make it as fantastic".

Carolin Rucks

"Every time I eat it I feel my stomach is alive again. I recommend it for those who are interested in those sensations".

Kernbaum Alexandre

"Raw Vegan Zen Lady's food is TOTALLY AMAZING! It's something that l have NEVER found anywhere. l have been eating the food for 5 years now. It is Super Special Food".

Roselyn Chari

Acknowledgments

I'd like to say thanks to my mom for being my biggest inspiration in the kitchen and probably my greatest teacher.

I'd like to thank my parents Bärbel and Klaus Bewilogua for making meals at our home an important part of our childhood, because it was the time we all got together as a family to enjoy food and each other's company.

Thank you Katrina Maclachlan for serving me my first Raw Pasta & Salsa. That meal really opened my eyes that Raw Vegan isn't just juicing and raw veggies.

Thank you my dear husband Philip Kneipp for pushing me to start writing my blog, and supporting me all the way through.

Thank you Roselyn Chari for being a patient student and helping in my tiny Tokyo kitchen.

Thanks to my beautiful twins Ethan and James for being patient with mommy.

Thanks to Tina Dose for taking the cover's photos and my 4-hour crash course on how to use a professional camera to shoot the food photos.

Thanks to my brother Thomas Bewilogua for designing Zen Lady's logo.

Thanks to Etsu Kahata for taking the photo of the Chocolate Dessert Flower Pot.

Thanks to Allan Appleby and Lee Bruce for editing the English.

Thanks to Jason Cottrell for the final proofreading.

Thanks to Keiko Ito for translating this book into Japanese.

The book was meant to be a bilingual paperback but unfortunately we had to go for Plan B and make the Japanese version an ebook.

Thanks to Dr Thomas N Lomax for suggesting a suitable title for the book.

And an extra big THANKS to Allan Appleby. If it wasn't for him I would have been lost in translation. He's the man that eventually worked on my photos and the layout.

Otherwise I'd like to thank my friends for sharing their recipes with me, tasting my food at my Raw Vegan Events and being great critics.

Preface

Ever since I can remember, I've loved to spend time with my mom in the kitchen.

Therefore a lot of recipes and inspirations originated from her and I veganised them.

I was born in 1972 in the former GDR. Early in my childhood I noticed how much impact certain foods can have on the body and mind. At age fourteen, I consciously stopped eating meat.

Before immigrating to the West in the late 1980s, I experienced a one year practicum as a cook.

Once we had moved to Hamburg, I completed a three year education to become a confectioner. This included the study of the chemistry of food and nutrition followed by a two year teacher's training.

After finishing my studies in Hamburg, I started working at the airport. Every day I would watch people travelling. Until one day I asked myself why I wasn't the passenger. I made the decision to pack up, leave everything behind and dare to jump into deep, unknown waters.

In 1996 I started my journey exploring the world and myself, taking up the teachings of Kundalini Yoga and learning about other cultures and their (eating) habits. I understood that animals and humans are all different with their own needs. Therefore I will not judge people that eat meat.

Having this knowledge I understand, that not everyone can be living on a Vegan or Raw Food diet.

As a person that lives and teaches yoga I encourage people to stay open minded, not to judge others and follow what is right for each individual's wellbeing.

I oppose animal cruelty and hunting for profit but I am not here to tell you to stop eating meat.

Whilst living in India, I learned about Ayurvedic wisdom (a traditional system of medicine in which illnesses are treated with a combination of foods, herbs, massage and special physical exercise). During my time in Israel, I gained a lot of knowledge of Kosher cooking, and whilst living in Ecuador, I experienced a diet consisting mainly of local fruits.

In 2006, the year that I became a certified yoga teacher, I also embarked on my first fully raw vegan diet.

My life changed when I met my husband in 2010 and gave birth to twins a year later. I had to learn how to prepare food for omnivores and integrate my raw vegan food.

Introduction

In this book you will find Zen Lady Hila's (Susanne Bewilogua) favourite RAW VEGAN dishes.

Raw Vegan Kitchen means simply that food isn't cooked. The Raw Vegan kitchen uses dehydration between 41 degrees and 48 degrees Celsius to withdraw water.

Occasionally people may steam or blanch their vegetables for a minute, according to their own taste.

Raw Vegan Kitchen soaks and sprouts instead of boiling.

But this book isn't only for people who love the Raw Vegan Kitchen.

My recipes could be the beginning of a slow transition from unhealthy processed food ingredients to homemade organic, more healthy nutritious meals without preservatives and unnecessary sugars.

Sadhana

Sadhana "A means of accomplishing something". Creating your personal Sadhana will work miracles in your life.

I've been through various stages in life. Such as starting to work as early as 5 am or commuting a long way to work by car or train. Travelling the world, having to deal with new environments or sickness. Working in three different jobs for sixteen hours a day, or eventually being a mom of twin boys.

I managed to cultivate a healthy routine and spiritual practice to enrich my life.

Once you're awake take a few deep breaths and smile, set a positive intention for your day.

Kundalini Morning Sadhana

- Tongue scraping.
- Rehydration.
- 5 minutes meditation.
- Concentrate on your Prana (breath).
- Concentrate on a Mantra (sound).
- Gaze at a Drishti (point of focus or a single object). This is called Dharana or "collection or concentration of the mind".
- Dharana will lead you to Dhyana (meditation) consciousness of the act of meditating.
- 15 minutes set of exercise and breathing.
- Yogic cold shower (Ishnaan).

My first Kundalini Yoga teacher Satya Singh in Hamburg once said "Even five minutes will make a significant difference in your life".

And he was more than right...

Cultivating morning rituals and practicing daily awareness will bring new wisdom every day.

Rehydration

In Japan, this method is used to treat various diseases. However, rehydrating your body is important in order for it to function well. The method prescribes drinking water right after waking up. I do, however, brush my teeth and scrape my tongue first thing in the morning. Afterwards, drink 800 ml of water. Don't eat anything for 45 minutes.

You may practice any form of cardiovascular exercise or Kundalini Yoga.

Tongue Scraping

Before even taking a sip of water, Ayurveda recommends we scrape away any white coating on the tongue. This coating is perceived as accumulated, undigested ama (toxins) lurking in the digestive tract. The scraping allows us to avoid ingesting this ama. Using a tongue scraper or metal spoon scrape from back to front and rinse the scraper after each scrape.

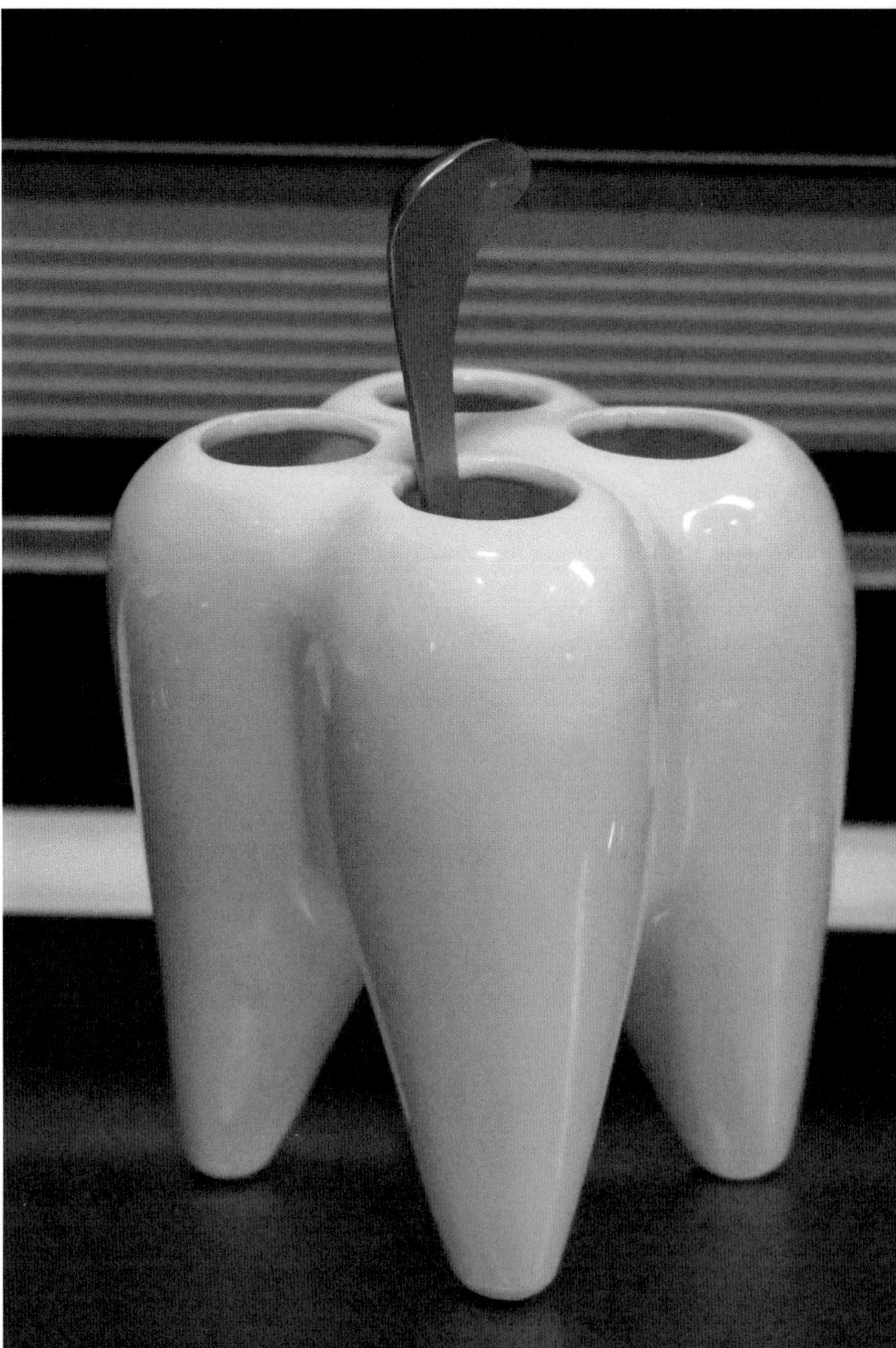

Using Neti Pot or Performing Oil Pulling

To get rid of any further lurking toxins, oil pulling is a great ancient Ayurvedic ritual that has numerous benefits.

Oil Pulling and Neti Pot can help:

- Reduce gum disease and inflammation.
- Enhance the senses.
- Increase clarity.
- Soothe a sore throat caused by pollen allergy, viral or bacterial infections.

Dry Brushing Skin

The skin is the body's largest organ and doesn't need to be stressed and overstimulated with soaps, shower gels, creams and oils in order to shine and glow.

I recommend brushing in the morning rather than at nighttime. Brushing has an incredible boosting effect and may keep you awake if performed before your nights sleep.

1. Start at your feet and brush upward towards the heart.

2. The chest area is where the lymph system drains. Similarly, when you start on your arms, begin at the hands and work upward.

3. Use firm, small strokes upwards, or work in a circular motion.

4. Brushing/Exfoliating helps to remove dead skin cells on the skins surface.

5. Have a warm shower to open pores and help to remove dirt.

6. Wash as usual, finish with a cold rinse, to help the pores close. It's important to rinse with cold water to prevent redness and swelling.

7. Your skin will look naturally beautiful and feel smooth and rejuvenated.

Alternatively, brush and oil your skin and use Ishnaan the magic cold shower and secret for health and beauty.

Ishnaan

"During hydrotherapy, the body is challenged by the cold water and by massaging the body, it can meet this challenge and not feel cold". -Yogi Bhajan

1. Dry brush your skin starting from your feet upward. If you are in a hurry, a few minutes will be enough. Remember less is more.

2. Massage your body with oil, such as sesame or any other Ayurvedic oil. This will prepare your body to warm up before the cold shower and leave your skin incredibly soft afterwards.

3. Best performed from 3 am to 8 am.

4. Shower cold. If you need to rinse with a bit of warm water, please do so but please finish off with cold water.

5. Rub and massage the body.

6. After a while you will feel yourself becoming warmer and warmer, then get out of the shower.

Rub yourself dry, your skin will have a healthy red colour. Immediately get dressed and put on warm socks.

Ishnaan or Yogic Shower Benefits

- Circulates blood to the capillaries.
- Cleans the circulatory system.
- Reduces blood pressure on internal organs, flushing them and giving them a new supply of blood.
- Strengthens the parasympathetic and sympathetic nervous systems.
- Contracts the muscles and causes them to eliminate toxins and poisons more quickly.
- Increases the power of resistance and resilience to the body.
- Strengthens the mucous membranes.
- Keeps the skin young and glowing.
- Prevents the body from developing an extra layer of fat, which affects the liver.
- Balances all the glands.
- Can help to relieve mild depression.

In the kitchen

Sprouting

Sprouting is the natural germination process by which seeds or spores put out shoots, plants produce new leaves or buds, or other newly developing parts experience further growth. In the field of nutrition, the term signifies the practice of germinating seeds to be eaten raw or cooked.

Dehydration

This applies for most goods that require dehydration, including pancakes, burgers, bread and cheese.

Preparing dehydrator meshes with dehydrator sheets (also called liners) is a good idea to prevent dripping.

For burgers, using shaping rings (optional) or hands, form burger patties of 90–100 g.

Dehydrate between 41–48 degrees Celsius for 2–3 hours.

Then, remove dehydrator sheets/liner and flip the food onto another dehydrator mesh.

If you left your food too long in the dehydrator, simply place them in an airtight jar or container and let them sit in the refrigerator to rehydrate.

The key is to experiment on your own regarding your personal food preferences.

Natural Colouring

Here some of the ways to give your food beautiful colour with natural ingredients.

Red/pink: beetroot, raspberry, blackberry and cranberry juice.

Yellow: saffron, turmeric powder or fresh turmeric roots.

Blue: blueberry juice, blue spirulina, blue-green algae powder.

Green: spirulina, chlorella, matcha powder, parsley, spinach, pandan leaves.

Black: charcoal powder, black sesame ground.

Brown: cacao, cinnamon, espresso.

Purple: red cabbage, blueberry juice, grape juice.

Orange: carrot juice or powder, paprika, saffron.

Dressings and Sauces

You may have purchased the most organic vegetables, the freshest salads and healthiest herbs, but if the dressing isn't delicious, your salad or veggies won't be tasty.

Arriving in Japan in the late 1990s, I immediately loved the way traditional Japanese meals were prepared: little dishes with just one mouthful of food. "What a genius idea!" I thought.

However, I always missed the simple, big, green salads on the menus.

Even back then, my choice were very restricted and I often felt helpless when trying to explain that I only eat vegetables.

"No, no meat please, no chicken, and sorry, no eggs and I don't like milk as well. No, I am not allergic; I just don't like it."

That was my standard speech when ordering food. Although I was practicing yoga daily, my way of eating was very unbalanced and not having enough intake of greens and fresh raw foods caused me to lose control of my body.

My standard breakfast was some oats with grated raw apple and carrot mixed up with soy milk.

I ate lots of rice with natto (sticky fermented soybeans), soba noodles, miso soup, konnyaku (made from a kind of potato starch), tofu, yuba, hijiki, seaweed, nori, and loads of raw fish.

One day, my dear friend Ben, visited Tokyo. He came over to my house to cook and really surprised me when he not only cooked dinner but also made his salad dressing from scratch.

He truly inspired me.

Always prepare for the next meal, and especially have salad dressing and other condiments ready. Have cut vegetables ready to go because we are often too hungry to spend time preparing them.

Recycling Citrus Fruit Leftovers

Citrus Fruit Leftovers

Citrus fruit as a natural deodorant are not only the cheapest but also healthiest alternative to common deodorants bought from a store.

Actually, you don't even need to cut a piece of citrus fruit, you just use the leftovers of the squeezed lemon, lime or yuzu you have in your water.

One little citrus fruit and so many uses. You know how it's said.

"There's a lesson in everyone you meet".

The "Lemon Lesson" I was taught in 1995 during my training to become a cooking coach.

I had to spend every afternoon in the office, doing the boring work of calculating and bookkeeping. I often I ended up chatting with the Chef-cook, a woman in her late 50s. She wasn't in such great body shape, but her skin was as soft as a newborn baby.

One day I asked her "What's your secret to such soft elbows?". She replied "Lemon!"

Every morning she would juice 1 lemon, then drink the lemon juice with water throughout the day.

Drinking lemon after meals helps with digestion.

She wrapped the empty halves around her elbows and knees. That helps the skin to stay beautifully soft and prevents dark dry cracks. (I am including my feet too.)

Once this was done she would use the lemon halves instead of toxic detergents to clean around the sink in her bathroom.

I made this my personal routine at home.

Recycling Coffee Grounds

Tips on How to Recycle Coffee Grounds

1. Place coffee grounds into the refrigerator to absorb odors. It works just like charcoal.

2. Use coffee grounds in combination with sugar to make a scrub to exfoliate your body. Leaves the skin deeply moistened.

3. Alternatively, make a mask for body and face.

Aloe Vera

Aloe Vera is an excellent treatment for skin conditions such as burns and eczema. It can also be taken internally.

Some of my smoothie recipes contain one or more teaspoons of fresh raw Aloe Vera. I used to have a whole family of Aloe Vera plants on my balcony, happily growing at almost 30 stories high, in the middle of Tokyo.

No matter what season, this powerful plant seems to survive rain, snow, typhoon storms and heat, including direct sunlight.

I have been including Aloe Vera in my diet for almost twenty years and there is much more to it than just eating it. The leftover skin can be perfect for treating little spots or wrinkles on one's face. It soothes sunburn and helps heal cuts, scratches and little wounds.

How to Prepare Aloe Vera

To trim and filete an Aloe Vera plant properly use a sharp knife.

Remove one of the outer leaves, which are the oldest and contain the most gel.

Wash your Aloe Vera leaf under running cold water and pat it dry, before cutting off the thorny edges. Whatever is leftover can be stored in a ziplock bag or airtight glass container in the refrigerator.

I like to prepare Aloe Vera in advance for medical use, so I freeze the Aloe Vera in an ice cube tray.

In this case, I will just cut the leaf into strips first and then into cubes, leaving the skin before freezing them. Whenever there is an emergency, they are ready to be used.

If your leaf is very small, you can cut it into halves, and using a teaspoon remove the raw Aloe Vera for your smoothies or salads.

始めましょう
Let's start

The Recipes

Breakfast Banana Pancakes 5
Cleansing Juice 7
Sourdough Bread from Pulp Leftovers 9
Detox Juice 11
Vitamin C Smoothie 13
Shiso Leaf Juice 15
Vegetable Juice 17
Flaxseed Pulp Leftovers Bread 19
Ashitaba Juice 21
Purple Magic Juice 23
Beautiful Skin Elixir 25
Limonana 27
Raw Milk 29
Beetroot Soup 31
Mom's Cold Cucumber Soup 33
Avocado Soup 35
Tomato Soup 37
Guacamole 39
Olive Spread 41
Cheese 43
Tomato Pesto 45
Mom's Basil Pesto 47
Grain Mustard Dip 49
Ketchup 51
Dill Dip 53
Shiso Leaf Dressing 55
Creamy Citrus Salad Dressing 57
Carrot Salad 59
Red Cabbage Salad 61
White Cabbage Salad 63
Fennel Salad 65
Egg Salad 67
Exotic Wild Rice Salad 69
Cucumber Noodles & Mint Sauce 71
Curry Sauce for Vegetable Pasta 73
Palak Paneer 75
Basic Raw Sushi Rice 79
Watercress Sushi 85
Tandoori Chicken 87
Knäckebrot 89
Onion Bread 91
Simple Ratatouille 93
Cream Cheese 95
Sunflower Cheese Ring 97
Camembert Blue Cheese 99
Tomato Cheese 101
Crispy Shiso Leaves 103
Masterpiece Lasagne 105
Twisted Grape Salad 109
Shiitake Burger 111
Indian Curry Burger 113
Mixed Mushroom Burger 115
Protein Burger 117
Carrot Dill Burger 119
Umeboshi Digestive Balls 121
Matcha Zen Energy Bites 123
Coconut Balls 125
Tutti Frutti Protein Bites 127
Chlorella Protein Bars 129
Cherry Blossoms Balls 131
Chocolate Dessert Flower Pot 133
Ice Pops 135
Chocolate Cake 137
Rule of Thumb for Chia Seeds 139
Sake Matcha Dessert 141
Kumquat Chia Seed Pudding 143
Butter 145
Banana Bread (dehydrated) 147
Tofu Spread 149
Beetroot Sülze 151
Black Rice Sprouted 155
Cauliflower Pakora 157
Ninja Power Cracker 159
Yogi Tea & Chia Seed Pudding 161
Salsa 163
Raw Vegetable Sushi 165
Spring Rolls 167
Cheddar Cheese 169
Whipped Cream 171
Ebi Dumplings 173
Pad Thai with Peanut Butter Sauce 175
Cucumber Pickles 177
Korean Style Kimchi 179
Marjoram Bread Spread 181
Extra Creamy Mayonnaise 183
Gazpacho 185
Broccoli Salad 187
Feta Cheese 189
Greek Salad 191
Watermelon with Feta 193
Raw Chocolate Bread 195
Heal Inside Out 197
Daikon Radish Salad 199
Cold Brew Coffee 201
Coffee Jelly Dessert 203
Tempura 205
Powerhouse Salad 207
Cucumber Avocado Rolls 209
Onion Steaks 211
Sprouted Quinoa Salad 213
A Glass Full of Goodness 215
Dairy Free Yogurt (CocoYo) 217
Vegetable Udon Noodle Soup 219
Charcoal (Frozen) Yogurt 221
Tropical Sprouted Black Rice 223
Chatzilim Aubergine Salad or Dip 225
Kombucha 227
Sauerkraut 229
Bitter Melon Juice 231
Potato Chips 233
Bondi Beach Salad & Chili Sesame Dressing 235
Breakfast and Dinner Smoothie 237
Beet Mood Salad 239

Be Happy

Breakfast Banana Pancakes

Ingredients

3/4 cup almond meal

1/4 cup almond milk

3 soft bananas, mashed

1 banana, cut into small pieces

Chia seed pudding, your choice

A handful of walnuts

Method

Combine all the ingredients.

Prepare a dehydrator mesh with a liner.

Using a tablespoon, spread the mixture in the shape of mini pancakes onto the mesh.

Dehydrate overnight at 41° C.

Serve with Whipped Cream (page 171) and maple syrup.

Cleansing Juice

Clean out and balance your ecosystem (microbiome).

Whenever you're busy, travelling or indulging in food that's usually not part of your regular diet, you may experience indigestion, bloating or other symptoms like allergic skin reactions on your face or other parts of your body.

There's no reason to panic; it just means your body is rejecting the unknown.

Knowing this will help you to stay calm and just heal and reset your inner ecosystem.

Ingredients

2 big tablespoons Sauerkraut (page 229)

1½ cups cherry tomatoes

2 carrots

Alternatively, simply juice the Sauerkraut, store in a container in the refrigerator and drink a shot in the morning or before bed.

Method

Using a slow/cold press juicer, make your Cleansing Juice.

Using a strainer, separate the pulp from the juice.

Keep the pulp to make Raw Vegan Sourdough Flat Bread (page 9).

Sourdough Bread from Pulp Leftovers

Ingredients

Pulp leftovers from Cleansing Juice (page 7)

½ cup chia seeds

1 cup water

2 tablespoons coconut flour

1 teaspoon sea salt

Method

Combine the water and chia seeds and set aside until the seeds absorb the water.

Make the cleansing juice and keep the pulp leftovers including the wet one after straining.

Combine all the ingredients.

Spread about 1 cup on each dehydrator mesh with liner.

This bread is so light that it doesn't need turning. It is ready to eat after about 5 hours.

Tip: *If your raw bread breaks into pieces store them in a jar and use as croutons in your soups.*

Detox Juice

This juice helps to detox your liver, fight belly fat and will make your skin glow overnight.

My first time away from Europe was when I travelled to San Francisco in March 1996.

When I spent time in the kitchen with Monika Dörning, she introduced me to fresh coriander. My absolute favourite herb in taste and smell.

I use coriander all the time, in sandwiches, as salads, for guacamole, in raw cheese, curries and as my daily secret skin enhancing and belly fat fighting elixir.

Drink about an hour before going to bed.

Ingredients

1 small cucumber

1 tablespoon fresh Aloe Vera

1 small tablespoon fresh ginger

1 bunch coriander

1 lemon, juiced

½ cup cold water

Method

Using a slow juicer, juice all the ingredients.

Add water and lemon juice.

Vitamin C Smoothie

Tokyo summers are so hot and sticky that it is hard to eat. Therefore, this quick to make smoothie with easy to purchase ingredients is a lifesaver.

Ingredients

1 big orange, peeled and pitted

1 big lemon, peeled and pitted

1 cup ice cubes

½ teaspoon turmeric, freshly grated

1 banana (optional)

Method

Using a blender, combine all the ingredients and drink immediately.

Shiso Leaf Juice

Ingredients

1 orange

½ apple

½ beetroot

10 shiso leaves

1 teaspoon apple cider vinegar

For Decoration

Ingredients

½ cup crushed ice

1 shiso leaf

Method

Using a slow juicer, juice the orange, apple, beetroot and shiso leaves.

Serve on crushed ice and add 1 tablespoon of apple cider vinegar.

Decorate with a shiso leaf.

Vegetable Juice

Inspired by my mom.

Every night before my mom goes to bed, she prepares the vegetables, so that they are ready to go into her slow juicer/cold press juicer first thing in the morning.

It makes me endlessly happy to see the transition from packed box juice to healthy, freshly squeezed juices.

Ingredients

1 small cucumber

1 stalk celery

1 big carrot

1 small piece ginger

1–2 apples

A few drops olive oil

Tip: *For a green version of this juice, add spinach, kale or Ashitaba.*

Method

Using a slow juicer, juice all the ingredients.

Using a strainer, separate the pulp from the juice.

Keep the pulp to make raw vegan flaxseed flatbread.

Flaxseed Pulp Leftovers Bread

Using the pulp leftovers of your juices is one of the smartest routines you can make a habit.

Ingredients

Pulp of the Vegetable (green juice) (page 17)

Including the leftover from straining, which will add some moisture to your bread

½ cup flaxseed

1 cup water

2 heaped tablespoons almond meal

1 flat teaspoon sea salt

Method

Combine the flaxseed with water and set aside for 1 hour or prepare overnight.

Once the water is absorbed and the seeds have expanded, add the other ingredients and combine.

Put about 1 cup onto a dehydrator mesh with liner.

Using a spatula or cake server, spread the mixture as thin as possible.

Dehydrate for 3 hours at 41° C.

Remove the liner and continue dehydration on the mesh for 6 hours or until the desired consistency.

Store airtight.

Tip: *If you love croutons in your soup, just break down this bread into small pieces.*

Ashitaba Juice

Ashitaba is also known as "Tomorrow's leaf" because when a leaf is harvested today, a new sprout grows overnight and is visible the following morning.

I discovered Ashitaba in 2006 here in Japan, and I have been using it in powdered form, cooked as a vegetable and raw for juicing or in salads ever since.

It is a tonic herb that has been revered for supporting beauty, such as: hair growth, nail and skin support, and longevity in Japanese traditional medicine for centuries.

It is also taken to support healthy cell regeneration, blood cleansing, digestion, skin care and as a mood booster.

Since the age of 6 months, my children have grown up on a daily glass of Ashitaba Juice.

Ingredients

1 bunch Ashitaba with stems

1 orange

8 freshly frozen grapes or pineapple chunks

1 small apple

1 small piece ginger (optional)

Method

Using a slow juicer, juice the ingredients.

Makes 1 glass of about 300–350 ml.

Using a strainer, separate the pulp from the juice.

Purple Magic Juice

Helps in weight loss. Red cabbage is very low in calories, but high in dietary fiber and has an abundance of important vitamins and minerals.

Ingredients

2 big apples

½ head small red cabbage

½ yuzu or orange, juiced

Method

Using a juicer, juice the apples and red cabbage.

Add the yuzu juice or citrus fruit.

Using a strainer, separate the pulp from the juice.

Serve on ice.

Beautiful Skin Elixir

This is the Queen of Infused Water

Ingredients

Fresh turmeric

Fresh ginger

Fresh mint leaves

Anise seed stars

Lemon to taste

Water

Honey to taste (optional)

Method

Wash the turmeric and ginger well, keeping the skin on.

Slice the turmeric and ginger.

Wash the mint leaves.

Squeeze the lemon.

Add all the ingredients to the water and chill in the refrigerator for 24 hours.

Limonana

In August 2000, I arrived for the first time in Israel.

I only stayed for 1 month in Israel, but it loved it so much that I decided to return to learn the beautiful language of Hebrew. This was the beginning of a long journey.

Beautiful women, handsome men on the beaches of Tel Aviv. Cafes along the shoreline. Sand under my feet, friends and laughter, Israeli music.

Rothschild Boulevard, Shuk' Ha'Caramel, Dizengoff, Ben Yehuda Street, Shenkin, Allenby Street, Yafo and Florentin... walks on warm summer nights... and LIMONANA: sexy, cool and super refreshing!

Ingredients

3 cups water

1 cup ice

3 lemons, juiced

3 tablespoons cane sugar, more to taste

¼ cup fresh mint leaves

Alternatively, for pure lemonade prepare without mint.

Method

Using a blender, blend all the ingredients on high speed.

Pour through a sieve into a glass carafe.

Chill in the refrigerator.

Alternatively, combine the water, lemon and sugar together.

Add fresh mint leaves and infuse the water overnight.

Serve on ice.

Raw Milk

Even as a child I didn't like milk. Little did I know, however, I instinctively started my first (food) diary in 1986. I would just make little notes about my weight, my skin and how I was feeling in general.

I noticed that eating dairy products made me feel unwell.

Ingredients

1 cup rinsed nuts or seeds, soaked overnight (shredded coconut, almonds, cashews, sunflower seeds, pumpkin seeds and rice are suitable). Oats and hemp seeds don't need soaking

3 cups water for thicker, creamy results or 4 cups water for thinner consistency

1 pinch Celtic or sea salt

1 pinch vanilla pod or extract

Sweetener to taste

Add natural food colouring or cacao powder (optional)

Method

Using a high speed or slow blender, blend until smooth.

Strain the milk through a cheesecloth or fine sieve.

Add the other ingredients.

Fill the ready to drink milk into a sterilised, airtight glass bottle.

Lasts for 1 week in the refrigerator.

Tip: *Nut milk pulp leftovers are delicious and can be immediately used for making yummy pancakes.*

Just add a couple of ingredients to the slightly wet nut pulp.

Beetroot Soup

Rich in iron, the beetroot helps the regeneration of blood cells.

Ingredients

1 big beetroot

3 stalks celery

3 large carrots

¼ cup lime juice

1 clove garlic, minced

1½ teaspoons sea salt

1 teaspoon caraway powder

1 bunch fresh dill

Method

Using a slow juicer, juice all the ingredients.

Using a strainer, separate the pulp from the juice.

Mom's Cold Cucumber Soup

This is one of my mom's unforgettable, delicious recipes that I remember eating throughout the year, whenever cucumbers were available.

It can be eaten just as a soup or added to other dishes.

Ingredients

7 small Japanese cucumbers

1 big clove garlic

1 teaspoon sea salt

1 tablespoon olive oil

¼ cup fresh lemon juice

½ teaspoon ground black pepper

1 cup homemade Dairy Free Yogurt (page 217)

1 bunch dill

Method

Grate the cucumbers with the skin.

Transfer to a serving bowl.

Combine the yogurt and other ingredients in a blender until creamy.

Pour over the cucumbers and chill in the refrigerator.

Add black pepper to taste.

Avocado Soup

I love this recipe because it's so flexible.

Take the recipe for guidance but feel free to add more or less of the ingredients to suit your preference.

Ingredients

2 bunches fresh parsley

1 lime, juiced

½ avocado

1 big tomato

½ cup cold water

3 ice cubes

1 tablespoon Tahini

2 tablespoons oregano

1 teaspoon sea salt

Black pepper, chili powder and cayenne pepper to taste

For Topping

Ingredients

Green onion

Hemp seeds

Method

Using a high speed blender, blend until smooth.

Top with green onion and hemp seeds.

Tomato Soup

Ingredients

1 cup cherry tomatoes

½ cup sun-dried tomatoes, soaked

1 lemon, juiced

3 ice cubes

1 tablespoon olive oil

1 pinch cayenne pepper

5 basil leaves

½ teaspoon sea salt

½ cup water

½ clove garlic, minced

For Decoration

Chives

Method

Blend all the ingredients together and serve.

Decorate with chopped chives.

Guacamole

Every party needs guacamole! I couldn't believe it when I heard people use artificial flavouring to make this simple dish.

This recipe is dedicated to my dear friend, Antonia. She finally made me write down the recipe, step by step.

Generally speaking, I love to prepare food by feeling and it was a big task for me to write down my recipes.

Having said this, please keep in mind that recipes are guidelines and inspirations. You need to adjust them according to your taste, adding salt or sugars, perhaps leaving out ingredients which are not to your preference or suitable for your body: including the knowledge of autoimmune disease, digestion hazards, intolerance or food allergies, stomach irritation etc.

Just be open minded and don't skip a recipe just because one ingredient doesn't work for you.

Ingredients

2½ avocados

2 tablespoons yellow onion, finely chopped

1 bell pepper, finely chopped

5 cherry tomatoes, quartered

1 bunch fresh coriander, finely chopped

1½ limes, juiced

½–1 teaspoon salt (Himalayan pink salt preferred)

1 clove garlic, minced

½ teaspoon chili powder

Black pepper

Method

Roughly mash the avocado.

Add all the other ingredients.

For more tasty results, let the flavours blend overnight.

Chill in the refrigerator.

Olive Spread

Ingredients

50 g pumpkin seeds

50 g sunflower seeds

2 cups black olives, pitted

2 bunches parsley

Sea salt to taste

1 tablespoon olive oil

Lemon juice to taste

Method

Using a food processor or fast speed blender, combine all the ingredients.

Lasts up to 2 weeks in an airtight container in the refrigerator.

You can use this spread to fill mushrooms heads and dehydrate them for 4–8 hours.

Tip: *For a seed free version, simply omit the seeds. It tastes just as good.*

Cheese

Learn this basic recipe and play around with flavours according to your taste.

Ingredients

1 cup nuts, soaked overnight (cashew nuts, sunflower seeds, pine nuts, walnuts or brazil nuts)

1 lime or lemon, squeezed

1 tablespoon Liquid Aminos or gluten-free soy sauce (Tamari)

1 clove garlic, minced

1 tablespoon Nutritional Yeast

Water or vegan milk for a more creamy consistency

Method

Using a fast speed blender, combine all the ingredients.

Enjoy this basic recipe.

For more variety, add your favorite herbs or veggies such as:

Coriander

Dill

Green/Red capsicum/Bell pepper

Chives

Mint

Black pepper

Olives

Onion

Beetroot

Capers

Tomato Pesto

Ingredients

1 cup sun-dried tomatoes

1 cup fresh mint leaves

¼ cup cashew nuts, soaked

2 tablespoons nutritional yeast

⅓ cup olive oil

3 cloves of garlic, minced

½ teaspoon sea salt

¼ teaspoon black pepper

1 pinch of red chilli flakes or more to taste

Method

Using a food processor or fast speed blender, combine all the ingredients.

Covered with a little extra olive oil, lasts up to 3 weeks in the refrigerator.

Can be used for pastas, bread spreads, cheeses or as a dip.

Mom's Basil Pesto

Before I even thought of making my own pesto from scratch, I used to empty all pesto jars from the refrigerator every time I visited my parents house in Germany.

One day, my mom gave me a gift. It was a handwritten recipe book with all my favourite dishes.

I simply veganised this recipe leaving out parmesan cheese and substituting with nutritional yeast.

Ingredients

40 g basil leaves

½ garlic clove, minced

20 g pine nuts

50 ml olive oil

1 dash lemon juice

1 pinch sea salt

1 flat tablespoon nutritional yeast

Method

Using a food processor, combine all the ingredients.

Covered with a little extra olive oil, lasts up to 3 weeks in the refrigerator.

Can be used for pastas, bread spreads, cheeses or as a dip.

Grain Mustard Dip

Ingredients

1 cup cashew nuts, soaked overnight

¼ cup lime juice

¾ cup fresh coconut water

1 garlic clove, minced

1 teaspoon sea salt

¼ cup old style whole grain mustard

Method

Using a blender, combine all the ingredients until smooth.

Lasts up to 2 weeks in the refrigerator.

Use as a dip, burger or vegetable topping.

Ketchup

Ingredients

1½ cups cherry tomatoes

⅛ cup apple cider vinegar or lemon

2 big soft dates or cane sugar to taste.

1 clove garlic, minced

1 pinch sea salt

1 cup soft sun-dried tomatoes (soak for 15 minutes if dry and hard)

Method

Using a blender, combine all the ingredients and blend until smooth.

Lasts up to 2 weeks in the refrigerator.

Use as a dip, for burgers, or a lasagna base.

For additional flavour when making the ketchup, add some onion.

Dill Dip

Ingredients

1 cup cashew nuts, soaked for 3 hours and rinsed

2 bunch dill with stems

¾ cup fresh coconut water

½ teaspoon sea salt

⅛ cup hemp seeds

⅓ cup lime juice

Method

In a blender, combine all the ingredients until smooth.

Shiso Leaf Dressing

This salad dressing is suitable for children due to the slightly sweet orange taste.

Ingredients

⅓ cup orange juice, freshly squeezed

2 tablespoons lemon or yuzu juice

1 teaspoon maple syrup

⅓ cup grapeseed oil

1 heaped teaspoon organic, white miso paste

1 pinch sea salt or Celtic salt

1 tablespoon apple cider vinegar

10 shiso leaves

Method

Using a fast speed blender, combine all the ingredients until green and smooth.

Lasts up to 2 weeks in the refrigerator.

Tip: *Tastes excellent on green salads.*

Creamy Citrus Salad Dressing

This recipe is my basic for most citrus salad dressings.

You can use Yuzu, Lime, Lemon or all three combined.

Ingredients

1/3 cup olive oil

1/3 cup citrus juice of your choice

1/2–2 teaspoons maple syrup

1/2 teaspoon sea salt

1 pinch black pepper

Method

Using a blender, combine all the ingredients and mix until creamy.

Lasts up to 2 weeks in the refrigerator.

Carrot Salad

This recipe was given to me by my dear friends and neighbours of Zenflat Nishi Azabu: Thomas and Miyoko.

Ingredients

2 carrots

1 clove garlic, cut into matchsticks

½ cup walnuts, soaked for 15 minutes

1 tablespoon olive oil

1 tablespoon lemon

½ teaspoon sea salt

Method

Ideally you would cut the carrots into matchsticks. I roughly grate them for time reasons.

Add all the other ingredients.

Use as a salad and topping, sandwich stuffing or as a filling in spring rolls.

Lasts up to 1 week in the refrigerator.

Red Cabbage Salad

Ingredients

½ head red cabbage

½ teaspoon sea salt

1 teaspoon olive oil

1 teaspoon red wine vinegar

¼ cup chives

1 pinch coconut sugar (optional)

Method

Using a mandoline slicer, slice the red cabbage.

Transfer the cabbage into a strainer and rinse under cold water.

In a bowl, add all the other ingredients and mix well.

Add the red cabbage and toss well.

Use for filling sandwiches and spring rolls or topping burgers.

For coleslaw salad, add Extra Creamy Mayonnaise (page 183).

White Cabbage Salad

Ingredients

½ small head white cabbage

1 teaspoon olive oil

1 pinch Celtic salt

1 teaspoon cumin seeds

Method

Using a mandoline slicer, slice the cabbage and transfer to a sieve to rinse.

Let sit to dry.

Transfer the salad into a plastic container, add all the other ingredients and shake.

Use for spring rolls, burgers and sandwiches.

Lasts up to 3 days. The longer you let the cabbage (red or white) sit, the more it ferments.

Fennel Salad

This recipe was given to me by my friend Erez. His family are originally from Yemen.

I lived with him and his sister in a small caravan in a Moshav in Israel for a while, before moving to Tel Aviv.

Whenever I make this salad, memories of sunlight and silence, singing birds and the sounds of spoken Hebrew return to my mind.

This salad is so delightful in taste and can also be used to fill up your vegan sandwiches.

Ingredients

2 small or 1 medium head fennel

½–1 lemon, juiced

½–1 teaspoon sea salt

2 tablespoons olive oil

1 pinch black pepper

Method

Using a mandoline slicer, slice the fennel.

In a container, add the sliced fennel and remaining ingredients, shake.

Chill for a few hours in the refrigerator.

Tip: *Salad leftovers can be placed into a blender. Adding some water makes a delicious light cold soup.*

Egg Salad

The Vegetables

Ingredients

6 small celery stalks

1 red capsicum (bell pepper)

¼ cup chives

The Dressing

Ingredients

2 cups cashew nuts, soaked for 3 hours

1 clove garlic, minced

¼ cup lemon juice

2 teaspoons turmeric powder

¼ cup water

1 teaspoon sea salt

Method

Cut the celery into 1 cm size pieces.

Chop the capsicum and chives into small pieces.

Set the vegetables aside.

Using a blender, combine all the ingredients for the dressing and blend until smooth.

Mix the vegetables with the dressing.

Add black pepper to taste.

Lasts up to 1 week in the refrigerator.

Exotic Wild Rice Salad

This salad is sensational! It takes a few days due to the process of sprouting, but in fact, it's a passive way of preparing this dish.

The Salad

Ingredients

450 g wild rice

1 kg frozen mango pieces

3 bunches coriander with stems removed

Method

Day 1: Put the wild rice into a sprouting jar. Cover with cold water. Rinse and change the water twice a day.

Day 2: Repeat.

Day 3: Repeat.

Important note: *Living in an Asian environment can be very challenging for raw food due to the potential of bad bacteria. I prefer to store my jar of rice from day 2 in the refrigerator.*

Day 4: Your rice is ready.

The Dressing

Ingredients

1/3 cup lime juice

1/3 cup grape seed oil

1 teaspoon maple syrup

1 pinch sea salt

Method

Drain the water and rinse the rice again.

Transfer the rice into a glass jar, then add the mango and coriander.

In a blender, make the dressing.

The dressing lasts up to 3 weeks in the refrigerator.

Serve on its own or with the Carrot Dill Burger (page 119).

Cucumber Noodles & Mint Sauce

Ingredients

8 Japanese cucumbers, spiralised

1 small, soft avocado

½ cup lime juice

2 stalks celery

1 cup mint leaves

½ cup hempseeds

½ teaspoon sea salt, more to taste

1 tablespoon chlorella powder (B12)

3 ice cubes

For Decoration

Sesame salt

Method

Using a spiraliser, make the cucumber noodles.

In a blender, combine all the ingredients and pour the sauce over the cucumber noodles.

Top with sesame salt.

Curry Sauce for Vegetable Pasta

This recipe is simply amazing because it tastes great with raw or blanched noodles.

The Vegetable Pasta

Ingredients

2 carrots

2 zucchini

2 yellow squash

The Curry Sauce

Ingredients

1 cup of cashew nuts, soaked for 3 hours

1 teaspoon olive oil

6 tablespoons lemon juice

½ teaspoon Himalayan pink salt

1 tablespoon Nutritional Yeast

1 clove garlic, minced

1 tablespoon curry powder

½ cup water

Method

Using a spiraliser, make the vegetable pasta.

Using a blender, combine all the curry sauce ingredients.

Pour over the raw pasta as much as desired.

Leftovers last up to 1 week in the refrigerator.

Can also be used as a dip.

Alternatively, bring water to a boil, throw in the vegetable pasta, turn off the heat and blanch up to 3 minutes.

Add ½ cup of broth to the curry sauce instead of water.

Palak Paneer

I spent many years travelling in India and this is my favourite veganised dish. Palak means spinach and Paneer means cheese.

The Spinach

Ingredients

300 g spinach, finely chopped

2 tablespoons coconut oil

1 tablespoon ginger, freshly grated

½ onion, cut into small pieces

1 bunch coriander, chopped

Method

Combine all the ingredients in a bowl then set aside.

The Cheese

Ingredients

2 cups cashew nuts, soaked at least 2 hours or overnight

6 tablespoons lime, freshly squeezed

1 teaspoon Himalayan pink salt

2 pinch coriander powder

2 pinch cumin powder

Method

Using a food processor, combine all the ingredients for the paneer until smooth.

Add the spinach mixture and pulse a few times to combine.

Can be stored in an airtight container for 1 week.

Tip: *Serve as a dip or with coconut wraps.*

For a vegan dish, cook Basmati rice and serve with raw Palak Paneer.

Basic Raw Sushi Rice

Ingredients

3 cups daikon radish

1 cup cashew nuts, unsoaked

½ teaspoon sea salt

2 teaspoons apple cider vinegar

Method

Wash, peel and cut the daikon radish into small cubes.

Using a food processor, add the daikon radish and cashew nuts and pulse a few times.

Add the sea salt and apple cider vinegar and process into rice-sized pieces.

Place into a sieve to get rid of excess liquid.

Watercress Sushi

Ingredients

1 pack small nori sheets (7 x 21 cm)

1 bunch watercress

3 shiitake mushrooms, sliced

Some cranberries

Method

To make the Basic Sushi Rice, follow instructions on page 79.

Place the nori sheets onto a cutting board or sushi mat.

Spread about 1 tablespoon of sushi rice onto each nori sheet.

Place the watercress, shiitake mushrooms and cranberries on each piece.

With both thumbs, lift up the edge of the sushi mat, the side closest to you.

Fold it over the ingredients and squeeze gently to keep everything inside (this takes some practice and patience).

Enjoy the sushi immediately.

Tandoori Chicken

When I was living in India and would eat out in restaurants, my friends' first choice would often be Tandoori Chicken.

I had to think of something to put on my party platter that comes close to chicken in looks and taste.

The Marinade

Ingredients

1 cup Dairy Free Yogurt (page 217)

3 tablespoons tandoori chicken spice

1 teaspoon fresh ginger, grated

1 teaspoon fresh turmeric, grated

1 teaspoon sea salt, more to taste

1 large carrot, finely chopped

1 lime, more to taste

1 tablespoon coconut oil

The Chicken

Ingredients

2 small heads of cauliflower

1 bunch coriander, finely chopped for decoration

Method

Make the marinade combining all the ingredients.

Wash the cauliflower and separate into small florets.

Coat the cauliflower with the marinade.

Prepare a dehydrator mesh with liner.

Place the cauliflower onto a tray.

Dehydration will take between 12–24 hours at 41° C.

When ready to serve, sprinkle fresh coriander over your Tandoori Chicken.

Knäckebrot

Ingredients

7 cups cauliflower florets

½ cup olive oil

1⅕ cups almond meal

1⅕ cups golden flaxseed meal

2 cups water

1 teaspoon sea salt

1 pinch cane sugar

⅓ cup chia seeds

Method

Using a food processor, process the cauliflower into floret-like pieces but not too mushy.

I recommend cup by cup.

In a bowl, combine the dry ingredients first then add the remaining ingredients.

Using a 18 x 18 cm frame, make it perfectly square.

Spread 1 cup of the mixture onto a dehydrator tray with liner.

Working quickly and evenly, distribute the mixture.

Dehydrate at 41° C for 12 hours.

Flip over on the mesh and remove the liner.

Using scissors, cut into pieces.

Dehydrate for another 12 hours.

Onion Bread

Ingredients

6 big yellow onions

1 big clove garlic, minced

1½ cups ground flaxseeds with mixed berries

¾ cup ground pumpkin seeds

¾ cup ground sunflower seeds

1 cup Amino Liquids

½ cup olive oil

1 pinch sea salt

Method

Using a mandoline slicer, slice the onion.

In a big bowl, combine all the ingredients.

Prepare dehydrator trays with tray liners.

Spread 1 cup (200 g) onion mix onto the tray about 5 mm thick. Continue until the mixture is finished.

Using a frame is optional.

Spread the mixture into a quarter-sized shape.

Dehydrate for 24 hours at 41° C.

Flip the bread over onto a tray mesh without the liner and continue dehydration for 12 hours.

Store up to 3 weeks in an airtight container.

Simple Ratatouille

The Tomato Sauce

Ingredients

1 cup cherry tomatoes

4 sun-dried tomatoes

1 tablespoon olive oil

1 clove garlic

¼ lime

Pepper and salt to taste

1 soft, large Medjool date or cane sugar

Fresh basil, oregano, marjoram, thyme

Herbs de Provence (dry herb mix)

Method

Using a blender, combine all the ingredients and blend until smooth.

Add fresh basil, oregano, marjoram, thyme and some Herbs de Provence (dry herb mix).

The Vegetables

Ingredients

1 red capsicum (bell pepper)

2 small aubergine (eggplant)

1 small zucchini

1 small yellow squash

1 onion, sliced

The Marinade

Ingredients

25 ml olive oil

1 pinch Celtic salt

Method

Cut the vegetables into mouth-sized big pieces.

Marinate the vegetables in oil and Celtic salt to taste.

Spread them out on a dehydrator mesh with liner.

Dehydrate at 41° C for 4 hours.

Transfer the vegetables into a glass bowl and add the tomato sauce.

Continue dehydration for 2 hours.

Cream Cheese

Ingredients

1 cup cashew nuts, soaked

1 lemon, juiced

1 flat teaspoon sea salt

Method

After soaking the cashews for 4 hours, drain and discard the water.

Place the cashews in a high speed blender.

Add all the other ingredients and blend on high speed until the cream cheese is smooth and creamy.

Store up to 1 week in an airtight container.

Add your favourite greens such as dill or chives (optional).

Or add Nutritional Yeast for a more cheesy flavour.

Use for vegetable rolls, bread, raw lasagna and dips.

Sunflower Cheese Ring

Ingredients

1 cup sunflower seeds, soaked overnight

4 tablespoons fresh lemon juice

4 tablespoons Tamari sauce

For Coating

1 tablespoon sunflower seeds

Method

In a food processor, combine all the ingredients, stopping occasionally to scrape down the sides with a spatula until well combined.

Place plastic wrap in a round-shaped mould.

Add the cheese.

Chill for 24 hours in the refrigerator.

Remove the cheese from the round-shaped mould and sprinkle sunflower seeds on top.

Dehydrate at 41° C for 24–48 hours.

Camembert Blue Cheese

Choose how mature you like your cheese to be. You can stop the dehydration after 48 hours or continue up to 72 hours or longer.

Ingredients

1 cup cashew nuts, soaked overnight

2 tablespoons Nutritional Yeast

½ teaspoon sea salt

⅛ cup vegan milk of your choice, more if needed.

Method

Using a blender, combine all the ingredients.

Stir well with a spatula until very smooth but not runny.

Place into a cheesecloth.

Place the cheesecloth into a straining dish.

Chill for 24 hours in the refrigerator.

The Blue Cheese

Ingredients

1 cup cashew nuts, rinsed

2 tablespoons Nutritional Yeast

1 teaspoon blue algae powder

½ teaspoon sea salt

1 clove garlic, minced

⅛ cup water

Method

In a blender, combine all the ingredients until smooth.

Place a 9 cm diameter serving ring onto a dehydrator mesh with liner.

Add half of the white cheese.

Add a layer of blue cheese and top with the rest of the white cheese.

Dehydrate for 24 hours.

Remove the serving ring and liner.

Continue dehydration for up to 72 hours or longer continuously at 41° C.

Chill in the refrigerator.

Top with almond flour.

Tomato Cheese

If you love sun-dried tomatoes, then you will love this cheese.

Ingredients

1 cup cashew nuts, soaked overnight

¼ cup soft sun-dried tomatoes (soak for 15 minutes if too hard)

1 tablespoon lemon juice

1 tablespoon Nutritional Yeast

¼ cup water

1 clove garlic, minced

1 pinch sea salt

Method

Using a blender, make the cream cheese first.

Then add sun-dried tomatoes and pulse.

The cheese should have visible pieces.

Place into a cheesecloth.

Place the cheesecloth into a straining dish.

Chill for 24 hours in the refrigerator.

The next day you will find the liquid has drained away from the cheese.

Can be eaten raw as a bread spread. Lasts up to 2 weeks in the refrigerator.

Alternatively, dehydrate.

Form the cheese into your desired shape.

Dehydrate for 24 hours at 41° C on a dehydrator mesh without liner.

Crispy Shiso Leaves

This Raw Vegan snack catches everyone's eye!

Ingredients

30 Shiso leaves

1 cup cashew nuts, soaked overnight

1 tablespoon Nutritional Yeast

½ teaspoon sea salt

1 tablespoon lime juice

½ clove garlic, minced

1 tablespoon onion, finely diced

For Colouring

Ingredients

⅛ cup beetroot juice

⅛ cup water + 1 teaspoon turmeric powder

Method

Wash the shiso leaves and let them dry on a towel.

In a food processor, make the raw vegan cheese.

Divide the cheese into 2 parts.

Combine the turmeric powder with water and add the mixture to 1 part.

Add the beetroot juice to the other part.

Using plastic gloves, cover 15 shiso leaves with the turmeric mixture.

Cover the other 15 shiso leaves with the beetroot mixture.

Place the leaves on a dehydrator mesh. Dehydrate for 12–24 hours.

Depending on the thickness of the leaves, very small and fragile leaves may only need 12 hours.

The bigger and thicker types need 24 hours for crispy results.

Store in an airtight container.

Masterpiece Lasagne

The Raw Vegan Cheese

Ingredients

½ cup lime juice

1 cup Liquid Aminos

1 clove garlic, minced

2½ cups sunflower seeds

Method

Using a food processor or fast blender, pulverise the sunflower seeds.

Add the remaining ingredients and blend until smooth.

The Tomato Sauce

Ingredients

500 g cherry tomatoes

¼ cup lemon juice

2 tablespoons Liquid Aminos

2 tablespoons olive oil

2 tablespoons onion, chopped

1 clove garlic, minced

1 cup soft sun-dried tomatoes

1 pinch sea salt

1 pinch cane sugar

1 tablespoon Herbs de Provence for flavour

1 bunch dill, chopped (added manually)

Method

Using a blender, combine all the ingredients and blend until smooth.

Manually add the dill.

The Pasta

Ingredients

3 medium zucchini

Method

Using a mandoline slicer, make the Lasagna noodles.

Set aside.

The Veggie Filling

Ingredients

1 medium beetroot (350 g), chopped into small pieces

12 small shiitake mushrooms, diced into small cubes

2 bell peppers, diced into small cubes

Method

For the dehydration, optionally use a frame (22 x 22 x 5 cm) for even layers and accurate form.

Combine the raw cheese, tomato sauce and veggie filling.

Make layers starting with the zucchini.

Dehydrate 12–24 hours at 41° C.

Excalibur

Twisted Grape Salad

It's time to play with flavours!

Ingredients

4 cups different coloured grapes

2 tablespoons fresh rosemary

1 lime, juiced

1 tablespoon raw honey

4 tablespoons olive oil

Sea salt to taste

Black pepper

¼ cup pine nuts

Method

In a salad bowl, make the dressing.

Mix with the grapes and add the pine nuts.

Shiitake Burger

Ingredients

18 shiitake mushrooms

2 tablespoons Tamari sauce

½ teaspoon smoked paprika powder

1 tablespoon maple syrup

1½ tablespoons apple cider vinegar

1 cup pumpkin seeds

½ cup carrots, chopped

⅓ cup celery, chopped

1 teaspoon fresh sage

Method

Using a clean, wet cloth wipe all visible dirt off the mushrooms and remove stems.

Using a food processor, chop the mushrooms into small pieces.

In a mixing bowl, make the marinade. Combine the Tamari, smoked paprika and maple syrup and whisk them together.

Add the chopped shiitake and set aside.

Using a food processor, process the pumpkin seeds roughly.

Remove from the food processor and set aside.

Chop the celery and carrots into fine pieces.

Combine all the ingredients.

Using a serving ring or your hands, shape into burger patties of about 90–100 g.

Place the burgers on a dehydrator mesh with liner.

Dehydrate for 2 hours, then turn, remove liner and dehydrate for another 4 hours or until desired consistency.

Lasts up to 3 days in the refrigerator.

Indian Curry Burger

Another perfect source of protein.

Ingredients

1½ cups almonds

1½ cups pecans

4 large carrots, medium chopped

1 medium red onion, medium chopped

1 bunch coriander, finely chopped

⅓ cup lime juice

1 teaspoon Himalayan pink salt

2 teaspoons dried rosemary

2 teaspoons dried tarragon

2 teaspoons curry powder

Method

Using a food processor, chop the nuts roughly then set aside.

Using a food processor, chop the carrots and onions.

Add all the other ingredients and combine until it is mixed well.

Using a serving ring or your hands, shape into burger patties of about 90–100 g.

Place the burgers on a dehydrator mesh with liner.

Dehydrate for 2 hours, then turn, remove liner and dehydrate for another 4 hours or until desired consistency.

Lasts up to 3 days in the refrigerator.

Tip: *Goes well with palak paneer, mayonnaise or ketchup.*

Mixed Mushroom Burger

Not all mushrooms are equal, therefore let's make a mixed mushroom burger. Alternatively, if you like a stronger taste, use portobello mushrooms only.

Ingredients

4 cups mixed mushrooms

2 tablespoons Liquid Aminos

¼ teaspoon dried thyme

¼ teaspoon dried rosemary

1 tablespoon maple syrup

1½ tablespoons lemon juice

½ cup sunflower seeds

½ cup pine nuts, roughly ground

½ cup carrots, chopped

⅓ cup celery, chopped

1 tablespoon fresh oregano

Method

Using a food processor, chop the celery and carrots into fine pieces.

Combine all the ingredients, pulsing gently but not into a mush.

Using a serving ring or your hands, shape into burger patties of about 90–100 g.

Place the burgers on a dehydrator mesh with liner.

Dehydrate for 2 hours, then turn, remove liner and dehydrate for another 4 hours or until desired consistency.

Lasts up to 3 days in the refrigerator.

Goes well with mayonnaise or ketchup.

Protein Burger

Unforgettably tasty!

Build on romaine lettuce, avocado, red caspicum (bell pepper), and cucumber slices topped with mayonnaise.

Ingredients

½ cup sunflower seeds, finely ground

½ cup pumpkin seeds, finely ground

½ cup hemp seeds

½ cup golden flax meal

2 teaspoons Herbs de Provence

1 teaspoon sea salt

1 cup red capsicum (bell pepper), chopped

1 cup celery, chopped

½ cup onion, chopped

Method

Add all the seeds, salt and Herbs de Provence to a mixing bowl.

Using a food processor, chop the vegetables one at a time using the pulse function.

Transfer to a mixing bowl to combine. Set aside for a few minutes.

Using a serving ring or your hands, shape into burger patties of about 90–100 g.

Place the burgers on a dehydrator mesh with liner.

Dehydrate for 2 hours, then turn, remove liner and dehydrate for another 4 hours or until desired consistency.

Lasts up to 3 days in the refrigerator.

Remember you need to experiment with your preference between raw, medium and well done results.

Tip: *If your burgers turn out too dry, store them in an airtight container in the refrigerator for 24 hours. This will rehydrate and blend all flavours perfectly.*

Carrot Dill Burger

This tastes best cold from the refrigerator with my exotic Wild Rice Salad (page 69).

Ingredients

4 cups carrots, chopped

1 clove garlic, minced

1–1½ teaspoons sea salt

2 tablespoons olive oil

¾ cup almond meal

½ cup golden flax meal

1 bunch dill with stems, chopped

Method

Using a food processor, chop the carrots.

Add all the other ingredients except for the dill.

Using the pulse function, combine well.

Transfer to a mixing bowl and add the dill.

Using a serving ring or your hands, shape into burger patties of about 90–100 g.

Place the burgers on a dehydrator mesh with liner.

Dehydrate for 2 hours, then turn, remove liner and dehydrate for another 4 hours or until desired consistency.

Lasts up to 3 days in the refrigerator.

Goes well with mayonnaise or ketchup.

Umeboshi Digestive Balls

These are excellent to finish a meal and help you digest your food. They are also super beneficial for an upset tummy.

Ingredients

1 cup gluten free oats, rolled

90 g ripe soft banana

½ cup umeboshi

3 soft dates, pitted

2 tablespoons coconut butter (not coconut oil)

For Coating

½ cup chia seeds

Method

In a food processor, combine all the ingredients until it forms into a ball.

Let the dough chill for 15 minutes in the refrigerator.

Put the chia seeds onto a tray. Using your hands form a zucchini-sized roll.

Cut into 1 cm pieces and form into little balls.

Place them on the tray with chia seeds.

Once you are finished making the balls, move the tray with both hands so the balls roll back and forth and are covered with chia seeds.

Lasts up to 14 days in the refrigerator.

Matcha Zen Energy Bites

Ingredients

1 cup cashew nuts, soaked for 8 hours

1 cup soft dates, pitted

½ cup cacao powder

1 tablespoon Matcha powder

1 tablespoon vegan milk

For Decoration

1 tablespoon Matcha powder

Method

In a food processor, combine all the ingredients until it forms into a little ball.

Prepare a small tray with plastic foil.

Place the dough onto the tray and refrigerate.

Cut into pieces when ready to eat as this is a faster method to make bars.

Sprinkle the Matcha powder on top.

Tip: *Alternatively, chill for 15 minutes in the refrigerator.*

Make a zucchini-sized roll and cut into 1 cm pieces.

Shape into balls then sprinkle the Matcha powder on top of the energy balls.

Lasts up to 14 days in the refrigerator.

Coconut Balls

Everything started with these coconut balls.

My friend Katrina is the person who truly inspired me to learn the art of making raw vegan food.

The Balls

Ingredients

½ cup almonds

½ cup pecans

½ cup walnuts

¼ cup dried apricots

¼ cup raisins

⅛ cup carob powder

⅛ cup cacao nibs

½ cup dried fruits such as:

Plums

Blueberries

Cranberries

Goji berries

For Coating

1 cup coconut, finely shredded

Method

Soak all the nuts for 3 hours.

Soak the dry fruits for 15 minutes.

Using a food processor, combine all the ingredients using the pulse setting.

With your hands form a zucchini-sized roll and chill for 30 minutes in the refrigerator.

Spread the coconut onto a tray.

Cut into 1 cm size pieces.

Make the balls.

Once all the balls are formed, gently move the tray with both hands to coat the balls evenly.

Tip: *Alternatively, spread dough onto a tray and make bars.*

Tutti Frutti Protein Bites

Ingredients

¾ cup coconut flour

2 cups cashew nuts, soaked for 8 hours

½ cup maple syrup

2 tablespoons white protein powder (I use Lucuma powder)

3 tablespoons colourful sprinkles

Method

In a food processor, combine all the ingredients, except for the sprinkles.

Pulse until well combined.

Add the sprinkles and combine manually.

Prepare a small tray with plastic foil.

Place the dough onto the tray and refrigerate.

Cut into pieces when ready to eat.

Chlorella Protein Bars

Ingredients

2 cups cashew nuts, unsoaked

½ cup cacao powder

1 tablespoon chlorella powder B12 (or Spirulina powder)

Extra powder for topping

1 cup soft dates

¼ cup dried candied yuzu or lemon

1 tablespoon vegan milk

Method

In a food processor, grind the cashew nuts.

Add all the other ingredients and combine until a ball forms. Use a spatula to occasionally scrape off the sides.

Prepare a small tray with plastic foil.

Place the dough onto the tray and refrigerate.

When ready to serve, cut into pieces.

Sprinkle chlorella powder on top.

Cherry Blossoms Balls

Perfect for your "Hanami" (Cherry Blossom) party to enjoy the beautiful Sakura trees with your friends and have something special.

Ingredients

1 cup cashew nuts, soaked for 1 hour

1 cup coconut, finely shredded

1 pinch sea salt

¾ cup soft dates

½ cup dried cherries

2 tablespoons Kirschwasser or sake

1 tablespoon beetroot juice for colouring

2 tablespoons cacao nibs

For Decoration

Ingredients

Pumpkin seeds

Coconut flour

Method

Using a food processor, combine the ingredients except for the cacao nibs.

Once the dough is formed, add the cacao nibs. Pulse once or twice only.

Form little balls and add the pumpkin seeds to decorate as a leaf.

Dip them into the coconut flour to decorate as cherry blossom dust.

Chocolate Dessert Flower Pot

This edible flower pot looks super fancy and time consuming, but in fact it's a quick, last minute option, if you need a stunning dessert.

Ingredients

4 large soft bananas

½ cup carob or cacao powder

2 big tablespoons tahini

1 drop vanilla or orange aroma oil (optional)

1 handful edible flowers of your choice

Method

Using a food processor, place all the ingredients inside (except the edible flowers) and process until smooth.

Transfer the chocolate pudding into a "Flower Pot". You can use any sort of glass container.

Decorate with flowers and chill for at least 30 minutes or longer.

Ice Pops

Ice pops are not only refreshing they are also easy to make.

Just blend your favourite fresh or frozen fruit and transfer it into an ice cream mould. Freeze them overnight.

If you're experimenting with a few flavours to make layers, you have to wait for about 30 minutes to add the next flavour. I like to use raspberries, mango and strawberries.

If you like to enjoy a scoop of sorbet or ice cream right away, use a food processor and break some frozen fruits, using the pulse function until creamy.

Optionally, add a little maple syrup and coconut yogurt.

Enjoy right away.

Ingredients for Simple Ice Pops

My favourites are:

Plain Mango

Plain Raspberry

Plain Strawberry

Plain Mixed Berry or in combination

For sorbet or ice cream, the following flavour combinations:

Pineapple + maple syrup + coconut yogurt

Banana + matcha powder + maple syrup + coconut yogurt

Mango + coconut yogurt

Chocolate Cake

The Base

Ingredients

1 cup almonds, or pecans, or pumpkin seeds or sunflower seeds

1 pinch sea salt

2 tablespoons cacao powder

2 tablespoons maple syrup

Method

Using a food processor, crush the nuts into very small pieces.

Add the cacao and salt and pulse for a few seconds.

Add the maple syrup and combine all the ingredients, pulsing until a ball-like shape forms.

Prepare a 15 cm springform circular or any round shape mould with clear foil.

Press the dough evenly into the bottom and sides of a springform pan.

The Filling

Ingredients

¾ cup coconut BUTTER (not oil)

¾ cup vegan milk of your choice (almond, oat or coconut milk)

¼ cup maple syrup

1 pinch sea salt

1 teaspoon vanilla essence

1 pinch vanilla pod

2 pinch espresso powder

¼ cup + 2 tablespoons almond butter

½ cup cacao powder

2 tablespoons cacao nibs

Method

Using a small blender, combine all the ingredients, except for the cacao nibs and blend until smooth.

Manually add the cacao nibs.

Transfer the filling into the springform pan.

Freeze cake for at least 8 hours or overnight. Tastes more delicious straight out of the freezer.

Defrosted it will become a Mousse au chocolat dessert.

Rule of Thumb for Chia Seeds

The rule of thumb is to mix 3 tablespoons of chia seeds to 1 cup of liquid of your choice.

A simple pudding, for example, could be to use 1 cup of homemade coconut, almond, soy or oat milk and 3 tablespoons of chia seeds.

Alternatively, you can try fruit juices, such as, blueberry or cranberry and 3 tablespoons of chia seeds.

Stir well and let sit for a few minutes, then stir again.

Chill in the refrigerator overnight. Lasts up to 1 week in the refrigerator.

Sake Matcha Dessert

For anyone who likes a little twist, this is the perfect dessert.

Ingredients

1 cup soy milk (homemade preferred)

4 tablespoons chia seeds

1/8–1/4 cup sake

2 tablespoons Agave nectar

1 teaspoon vanilla extract

1 pinch vanilla pod

For Decoration

Ingredients

Matcha powder

Edible white flowers

Method

Place all the ingredients into a small bowl and stir together.

After about 2 minutes, the chia seeds start to absorb the liquid and the dessert begins thickening.

Using a funnel, divide the dessert into small portions.

Chill in the refrigerator for 8 hours or longer. Lasts up to 5 days in the refrigerator.

When ready to serve, sprinkle Matcha powder on top and decorate with a white flower.

Kumquat Chia Seed Pudding

Ingredients

1 cup almond milk

3 tablespoons chia seeds

1 teaspoon orange extract

1 tablespoon maple syrup

10 kumquats

For Decoration

Shiso leaves

Method

Make the Chia Seed Pudding and let it rest for 1 hour in the refrigerator.

Cut the kumquats into very fine slices.

Make sure your glasses are clean and dry from inside so the kumquat slices will stick to it.

Fill it up with pudding and decorate with shiso leaves.

Butter

Ingredients

50 g cacao butter

150 ml rapeseed oil

1 pinch sea salt

Method

Put the cacao butter into a stainless steel bowl.

Place this bowl into a larger pot with hot water.

Let the cacao butter melt.

Add the sea salt and slowly stir the rapeseed oil into the cacao butter.

Transfer it to a glass or ceramic container.

Let it chill overnight in the refrigerator.

Lasts for 2 weeks in the refrigerator.

Banana Bread (dehydrated)

Ingredients

½ cup walnuts, soaked overnight

1 cup almonds, soaked overnight

½ cup pecans, soaked overnight

1 cup dried banana chips

¼ cup carob powder

7 medium-sized ripe bananas

½ cup hand-cut dried figs (in rings)

1 pinch Himalayan pink salt

¼ teaspoon fresh vanilla pod

½ teaspoon cinnamon powder

Method

Using a food processor, grind the dried bananas.

Add the nuts, carob powder and spices.

Transfer it to a bowl.

Mash or blend the bananas.

Combine the dry and wet ingredients. Put the hand-cut figs directly onto a dehydrator mesh with liner.

Add 2 cups of the dough and spread out evenly. Makes 4 breads.

Dehydrate for 6 hours at 41°C, then flip over, remove liner and continue dehydration until the desired firmness (up to 24 hours).

Lasts for 2 weeks in the refrigerator.

Tofu Spread

I spent an autumn and winter in Osaka. This simple Vegan bread spread is not raw but I love tofu, therefore I love to share it.

I was given this recipe by my friend Veli.

Ingredients

1 block hard tofu

1 large carrot, finely grated

1 tablespoon olive oil

1 tablespoon onion, finely cut

1 tablespoon chives, chopped

½ teaspoon sea salt

Method

Remove the tofu from the container and dry it using a cotton cloth or kitchen paper.

Combine all the ingredients.

Lasts up to 3 days in the refrigerator.

This is also the filling for my Ebi Dumplings (page 173).

Beetroot Sülze

I fell in love with this dish the first time my mom made it and I veganised it. Sülze stands for jellied meat.

The Raw Cream Cheese

Ingredients

(You can also use Feta Cheese - page 189)

2 cups cashew nuts, soaked overnight

6 tablespoons lemon juice

4 tablespoons nutritional yeast

¼ teaspoon sea salt

1 pinch black pepper

Water if needed

15 g washed and rinsed Irish moss, soaked in hot water for 15 minutes

1 bunch dill with stems, chopped

Method

In a food processor, combine all the ingredients, except for the dill, and combine until smooth.

Remove from the food processor.

Using a spatula, add the dill to the cream cheese.

Set aside to chill in the refrigerator.

The Beet Sülze

Ingredients

Use Irish moss to make 4 raw patties.

1 cup beetroot juice

½ teaspoon Celtic salt, more to taste

½ teaspoon apple cider vinegar

½ teaspoon cumin powder

120g Irish moss washed and rinsed with extra care to remove dirt, and soaked 24–48 hours in cold water

Method

Place Irish moss into hot water and let expand for 15 minutes.

Drain the water and transfer Irish Moss and all other ingredients to a blender. Gently blend until a gel forms.

Transfer into 4 serving rings and chill for 20 minutes in the refrigerator.

Once the beet has settled, add the cream cheese or feta cheese and chill the Sülze for 8 hours. When ready to serve, remove from rings or bowl.

Sea Moss

Sea moss is a type of algae which grows on the rocky parts the Atlantic coast and North America.

It is referred to by several names including Irish moss, Chondrus Crispus and Carrageen moss.

Wash, soak and use for drinks, smoothies, desserts, cakes, ice creams and much more as a substitute for gelatin.

Black Rice Sprouted

Ingredients

1 cup sprouted rice (follow instructions for Exotic Wild Rice on page 69)

1 cup carrots, diced

1 cup red capsicum (bell pepper), diced

1 cup cucumbers, diced

1 cup celery, diced

1 bunch tablespoon coriander

The Dressing

Ingredients

2 tablespoons umeboshi vinegar

2 tablespoons lime oil

1 teaspoon fresh turmeric root, grated

1 clove garlic, minced

1 teaspoon sea salt

Black pepper

Method

Soak and rinse the black rice 3 times daily for 3 days.

Sprout and rinse twice daily for another 3 days.

Finely dice all the vegetables.

In a salad bowl, make the dressing and stir well.

Add the sprouted rice and vegetables.

Let the salad chill in the refrigerator for a few hours or overnight to absorb the dressing.

Tip: *If blueberries are in season, add 1 cup to boost the nutritional value.*

Cauliflower Pakora

This Indian inspired dish is simple and delicious.

Ingredients

1 head cauliflower

Coconut or sesame oil

Method

Break the cauliflower into florets, sprinkle with some Himalayan pink salt, and let sit for 15 minutes.

Rinse the cauliflower.

Marinate the cauliflower in coconut or sesame oil and put into a dehydrator for 2 hours.

That way the Pakora will be soft inside and crispy outside.

Pakora Tomato Batter

Ingredients

2 cups cherry tomatoes

10 sun-dried tomatoes

1 onion, diced

Big handful of coriander, chopped

Himalayan pink salt

¼ teaspoon black pepper

¼ teaspoon turmeric powder

¼ teaspoon fennel seed powder

¼ teaspoon red chilli powder

1 Medjool soft date

Method

Blend the ingredients for the batter until smooth.

Remove the cauliflower from the dehydrator and coat with the batter.

Dehydrate again for 24 hours.

Serve with lime and fresh coriander.

Ninja Power Cracker

Ingredients

1 cup chia seeds

1 tablespoon charcoal powder

1 teaspoon Celtic salt

¼ cup black sesame seeds

2 cups water

For Topping

Sesame salt

Method

In a mixing bowl, combine the dry ingredients.

Add to water and stir well.

Let expand for 10–15 minutes.

Prepare a dehydrator mesh and liner.

Using a spatula, spread the mixture onto the mesh about 2 mm thick.

Sprinkle a little sesame salt on top.

Dehydrate for 4 hours at 41° C.

Flip over and remove the liner.

Using scissors, cut the cracker into squares.

Continue to dehydrate a further 8 hours or longer for a more crispy consistancy.

Store in an airtight container.

Yogi Tea & Chia Seed Pudding

Whenever I miss India, I prepare Yogi Tea. You don't need to buy expensive or fancy Yogi Teas, if you love Yogi Tea or Chai as much as I do.

The five traditional Ayurvedic spices: cardamom seed, cinnamon bark, clove bud, ginger root and black pepper are available everywhere.

I add homemade almond or coconut milk and sweetener.

Ingredients

1 liter water

4 cinnamon sticks

6 cardamom seeds

1 teaspoon cloves

20 pepper corns

1 big piece fresh ginger

1–2 black tea bags

Method

Bring the water to a boil, add ingredients and steep for 20 minutes or longer.

Proceed with making Chai Tea by adding milk.

For chia seed pudding follow the Rule of Thumb recipe on page 139.

Salsa

Inspired by Katrina MacLachlan

Ingredients

2 cups sun-dried tomatoes, soaked in 1 cup of olive oil

1 teaspoon white miso paste

1 tablespoon Tamari

½ lime, juiced

½ teaspoon sea salt

Water if needed to make tomato base smooth

Raw honey to taste

2 cups red bell pepper, finely chopped

1 chili or jalapeno, chopped small

1 cup cherry tomatoes, finely chopped

1 cup cucumbers, finely chopped

1 tablespoon onion, finely chopped

1 clove garlic, minced

Coriander or chives

Method

Using a high speed blender, combine the sun-dried tomatoes with oil, miso paste, Tamari, honey, lime and sea salt and make the tomato base.

Add the chopped vegetables.

Use for dipping, raw salads, raw vegetable pasta etc.

Tip: *Serve with raw or balanced spiralised zucchini vegetable pasta.*

Alternatively, using a mandoline slicer, slice zucchini into flat strips and dehydrate for a few hours.

Raw Vegetable Sushi

Here comes the reason why you should always have some cut veggies ready to go in your refrigerator.

Let's be honest, the reason why many people often end up eating unhealthily, is that they don't have the time or energy to prepare proper nutritious food when they are already feeling very hungry.

So, let's make the effort to cut a handful of our favourite veggies twice a week and box them up.

Ingredients

1 small cucumber, cut into 8 sticks

¼ small head red cabbage, finely shredded

¼ beetroot, cut into matchsticks

½ red bell pepper, cut into sticks

8 romaine lettuces

1 avocado mashed with juice of lime, salt, black sesame and fresh broccoli sprouts

8 Nori sheets (19 x 6.5 cm)

Add your favourite raw vegan cheese (optional)

Method

Lay a nori sheet onto a tray.

Place the romaine lettuce leaf on top.

Add 1 teaspoon of the avocado mixture.

Add the remaining ingredients and roll up.

Enjoy with gluten-free soy sauce, Tamari sauce or Liquid Aminos.

Spring Rolls

I love spending time in Vietnam and Thailand. One dish I truly appreciate are fresh spring rolls.

To make spring rolls, use the salad recipes from this book or simply use fresh raw vegetables. There are endless possibilities. You can use most of the dips or just use Tamari to add flavours to your raw veggies.

Cheddar Cheese

Ingredients

1 cup cashew nuts, soaked overnight

1 lime, juiced

1 big red paprika

1 teaspoon sea salt

Method

Using a fast speed blender, combine the ingredients except for the Nutritional Yeast.

(Here you can stop and already use the spread as a paprika cream cheese).

Let sit in a straining dish in the refrigerator for 24 hours.

Shape the cheese into a square about 1 cm thick.

Coat with the Nutritional Yeast and place in a dehydrator.

Dehydrate at 41° C.

After 24 hours remove the liner and continue dehydration up to 72 hours.

Top with Nutritional Yeast to dehydrate.

Whipped Cream

Ingredients

Flesh of 1 coconut

Pure water

Method

Using a fast speed blender, combine the ingredients until super creamy.

Serve with fruits, cakes or pancakes.

Ebi Dumplings

Ingredients

1 recipe Tofu Spread (page 149)

½ recipe Peanut Butter Sauce (page 175)

6 rice paper

Green onion

Method

Cut the rice paper into quarters.

On a big plate, put warm water.

On a second plate, stretch a plastic food wrap over the edges. This will help to shape and remove the little dumplings effortlessly.

Soak ¼ rice sheet until soft. Fill with tofu spread.

Each dumpling is about 1 teaspoon of tofu spread.

Twist to close.

Sprinkle the green onion on top and serve with the peanut butter sauce and gluten-free soy sauce (Tamari).

Pad Thai with Peanut Butter Sauce

This sauce is for raw vegetables and pastas of any kind. My favourite is 4 spiralised carrots, blanched for 3 minutes.

It makes a delicious dip for spring rolls and a fantastic salad dressing.

Ingredients

⅓ cup warm water

½ cup peanut butter

⅛ cup Tamari or Liquid Aminos

1 tablespoon ginger, grated

½ clove garlic, minced

2 tablespoons apple cider vinegar

1 tablespoon sesame oil

Chilli, cayenne pepper, black pepper and sea salt to taste

1 teaspoon raw honey or 1 soft date

Method

Combine all the ingredients and blend until smooth.

If you blanched the vegetable pasta, use ⅓ cup broth instead of plain water.

Cucumber Pickles

When I was little, my mom used to make these "Ostdeutsche Schnellgurken" (cucumber pickles) whenever we had the possibility of purchasing cucumbers, which was not a common vegetable on East German shelves.

Ingredients

1 kg cucumbers, peeled

2 teaspoons salt

2 tablespoons white sugar

1–2 small white onions, chopped

10 black peppercorns

2 tablespoons mustard seeds

1 bunch dill

Method

Cut the cucumbers in 2 cm big pieces.

In a container, add all the other ingredients and shake.

Chill in the refrigerator for 8 hours.

Korean Style Kimchi

Ingredients

1 kg Chinese cabbage (reserve 2 outer leaves of the cabbage)

¼ cup salt

Water (for soaking cabbage)

The Marinade

Ingredients

6 cloves garlic

3 tablespoons Korean style red pepper flakes (Gochugaru)

2 tablespoons Tamari

2 teaspoons brown sugar

3 pieces ginger, 5 mm thick

The Vegetables

Ingredients

½ cup red bell pepper, finely sliced

2 cups daikon, cut into matchsticks

1 bunch scallions, finely chopped

Method

Cut the Chinese cabbage into 1 cm thick pieces.

Put the cabbage into a bowl with cold water and add ½ cup salt. Cover with a plate. Let sit to soak for 6 hours.

Using a food processor, or a fast speed blender, combine all the ingredients to make the marinade and blend well.

Chill in the refrigerator.

Using a knife, cut the vegetables and rinse and drain the cabbage very well.

In a bowl, combine the cabbage and vegetables with the marinade. (Using gloves is advised.) Toss well.

Put the cabbage mixture into a fermentation pot.

Place the reserved cabbage leaves on top, add fermentation weights, and press down. The leaf and weights will help keep the cabbage submerged.

Let sit at room temperature for 3 days.

Transfer to the refrigerator and continue the fermentation for at least 2 weeks so flavours will blend in well.

Marjoram Bread Spread

Ingredients

1 bunch fresh marjoram

1 small onion

1 garlic clove, minced

¼ cup hazelnuts

¼ cup sunflower seeds

¼ cup pumpkin seeds

1 tablespoon gluten-free soy sauce

2 tablespoon olive oil

2 tablespoons whole grain Dijon mustard

Pepper, salt and paprika to taste.

Method

Using a food processor combine all the ingredients.

Lasts up to 2 weeks in the refrigerator.

Extra Creamy Mayonnaise

Ingredients

1 cup cashew nuts, soaked for 3 hours

¼ cup lemon juice

¾ cup fresh coconut water

1 garlic clove, minced

1 teaspoon sea salt

¼ cup Dijon Grey mustard

Method

Using a blender, combine all the ingredients until smooth.

Lasts up to 2 weeks in the refrigerator.

Use as a dip, burger or vegetable topping.

Gazpacho

My first trip to Spain in 1990 was filled with culinary experiences and I fell in love with this classic recipe.

Ingredients

1 cup cucumber, diced

1 cup celery, diced

1 cup red paprika, diced

4 medium-sized tomatoes, diced

2 jalapeno peppers, chopped

¼ cup green onion

Method

Let vegetables sit aside in a bowl.

The Tomato Sauce

Ingredients

500 g cherry tomatoes

¼ cup olive oil

¼ cup lime juice

2 tablespoons gluten-free Worcester sauce

1 big clove garlic, minced

½ teaspoon dried oregano

½ teaspoon black pepper

1 teaspoon sea salt, more to taste

½ teaspoon cayenne pepper

½ teaspoon cumin powder

Method

Using a blender, combine all the ingredients and blend well.

Pour the tomato sauce through a strainer/sieve into 2nd empty bowl.

Take about ⅓ of the vegetables and put into the blender.

Add the tomato sauce and blend.

Pour the entire vegetable tomato sauce over the vegetables and chill.

Broccoli Salad

Ingredients

1 serving Extra Creamy Mayonnaise (page 183)

¼ cup vegan milk

2 small heads broccoli

1 small red onion, chopped

¼ cup raisins

½ cup pine nuts

Balsamic vinegar, salt and pepper to taste

Method

Wash the broccoli.

Separate the florets.

Make the dressing.

Combine all the ingredients.

Alternatively, steam the broccoli for a few minutes.

ZEN LADY
http://rvztokyo.com/

Feta Cheese

Ingredients

200 g almonds

½ cup freshly squeezed lemon

¼ cup olive oil

1 big clove garlic, minced

1½ tablespoons sea salt

Method

Pour hot water over the almonds. After 10 minutes peel off the skin.

Using a food processor, combine all the ingredients.

In a straining dish, chill in the refrigerator for 24 hours.

Using a scoop, serve the feta cheese.

Alternatively, squeeze out the excess water with a cheesecloth and chill the feta for 48 hours in the refrigerator. Then cut the feta into cubes (optional).

Greek Salad

Ingredients

1 serving of Feta Cheese (page 189)

1 red capsicum (bell pepper)

1 cup black olives

2 small cucumbers

1 small onion

1 cup yellow or red cherry tomatoes

The Dressing

Ingredients

2 tablespoons of olive oil

1 tablespoon lemon juice

½ teaspoon sea salt

1 teaspoon dried oregano

Method

Cut the vegetables into mouth-sized pieces.

Slice the onion into rings.

Combine all the ingredients for the dressing until creamy.

Mix the vegetables in a salad bowl and toss with the dressing.

Watermelon with Feta

If you're feeling hot and exhausted, just get some watermelon and put a little piece of feta onto it. I brought this recipe back from Israel.

The combination of water and salt supplies the body with enough minerals during hot summer days.

Ingredients

¼ watermelon

½ block Feta Cheese (page 189)

Raw Chocolate Bread

This recipe is the raw answer to a fruit loaf.

Ingredients

1 cup pecans, soaked for 1 hour

1 cup walnuts, soaked for 1 hour

¼ cup cacao powder

3 heaped tablespoons almond butter

2 tablespoons maple syrup

6 dried figs, soaked

⅛ cup cacao nibs

Method

Prepare a baking bread pan (17 x 8.5 cm) with plastic foil.

Place the cacao nibs on the bottom of the pan or mould.

Using a food processor, grind the nuts and cacao powder together.

Add all the other ingredients and combine until a ball forms.

Remove from the food processor and place into the mould.

Flip the pan/mould upside down and remove the foil.

This is raw chocolate bread and can be enjoyed right away.

Keep in the refrigerator.

Heal Inside Out

This recipe is especially beneficial when in need of antibiotics or battling yeast overgrowth, also known as Candida, which is very common.

This recipe has antifungal and antibacterial properties.

I highly recommend it whilst taking a course of antibiotics or other medications.

(Sometimes conventional medicine is necessary when natural remedies are not working).

Ingredients

200 g onions, finely diced

300 g apples, roughly grated

70 g hazelnuts, roughly chopped

1 big clove garlic, finely minced

1 bunch fresh sage, chopped

1 bunch fresh oregano, chopped

1 teaspoon lemon juice

Black pepper and sea salt to taste

Method

In a food processor, combine all the ingredients.

Carefully pulse only a few times.

Lasts up to 1 week in the refrigerator.

Daikon Radish Salad

Ingredients

3 cups daikon radish, roughly grated

1 cup cherry tomatoes, cut into halves

1 lime, juiced

1 tablespoon olive oil

½ cup Dairy Free Yogurt (page 217)

Pepper and salt to taste

For Topping

Chives

Method

Make the dressing.

Add the daikon radish and tomatoes.

Top with chives.

Cold Brew Coffee

The first evidence of true cold-brewed coffee, made with cold water, comes from Kyoto, Japan. The Japanese were brewing coffee this way already in the 1600s.

Ingredients

1 cup whole coffee beans

4 cups pure or filtered water

Pinch sea salt

Method

Grind the coffee beans on the coarsest setting, using the pulse function.

Transfer the coffee grounds to a glass container.

Pour the cold water over the top.

Stir gently with a long-handled spoon to make sure the grounds are thoroughly saturated with water.

Cover the jar with a lid.

Chill for 8–12 hours on the kitchen counter.

Using a strainer, transfer the coffee into a glass carafe and chill in the refrigerator.

Coffee Jelly Dessert

When I arrived in Japan in 1998, I immediately fell in love with coffee jelly.

It helped me to overcome my sweet cravings.

Here's my veganised version of it.

Ingredients

2 cups Cold Brew Coffee (page 201)

⅓ cup vegan milk

1 tablespoon peanut or almond butter

2 tablespoons maple syrup

1 pinch vanilla pod

10 tablespoons chia seeds

For Topping

About 300 ml vegan milk

Method

Using a blender, combine the coffee, almond or peanut butter, maple syrup, milk and vanilla.

Transfer the liquid into a jar, add chia seeds and stir to combine.

Let the mixture sit for a few minutes, stir again and then transfer into small glasses.

Chill in the refrigerator overnight.

Top with milk.

Lasts up to 5 days in the refrigerator.

Tempura

The Tempura Coating/Batter

Ingredients

2½ cups water (more if needed)

1½ tablespoons golden flaxseed meal

1 teaspoon sea salt, more to taste

⅔ cup ground buckwheat

The Vegetables

Ingredients

1 red capsicum (bell pepper)

1 small zucchini

Shiitake mushrooms

Sesame oil for marinade

Method

Wash and cut the vegetables into mouth-sized pieces.

For the batter, combine water and golden flax meal and set aside for 10 minutes.

Grind the buckwheat grains and add the sea salt.

Combine the wet and dry ingredients.

Experiment with the coating batter thickness.

Coat the vegetables in the batter and place on the dehydrator mesh with liner.

Dehydrate between 4–15 hours depending on your crispiness preference.

Serve with salt or other condiments or on top of udon soup

Powerhouse Salad

This salad can be enjoyed by everyone at any time, especially during hot summer days.

I created this recipe when I was suffering from extreme migraines and nausea.

Ingredients

1 small bunch spinach, stems removed, cut small

1 tablespoon coconut oil

½ lemon, juiced

½ teaspoon raw honey

1 pinch of Himalayan pink salt

1 heaped cup cubed watermelon

1 teaspoon ginger

¼ cup mint leaves

½ cup blueberries

1 tablespoon sesame seeds

2 tablespoons gluten-free oats

¼ cup almonds

Method

In a small blender or using a whisk, combine the coconut oil, lemon juice, honey and salt until creamy.

In a salad bowl, toss spinach with the dressing.

Add all the other ingredients and enjoy immediately.

Cucumber Avocado Rolls

Ingredients

Guacamole (page 39) Add a little chili powder

Nori sheets

Japanese cucumbers

Sesame salt

Method

Make the guacamole.

Using a mandoline slicer, slice the cucumbers into long flat pieces (along the length).

Place the cucumbers onto a tray.

Cut the nori sheets into long, rectangular pieces about the same width and length as the cucumber and place on top.

Using a pastry bag, spread the guacamole along the layered cucumber and nori.

Shape into a roll.

Sprinkle with sesame salt.

Onion Steaks

Ingredients

2 big red onions

1 Feta Cheese (page 189)

Olive oil for moisture

Beetroot juice for colouring (optional)

Method

Make the feta cheese and add a little water for a more creamy consistency.

Peel the onions and slice into 1 cm thick rings.

Using a spatula, coat the onion rings with feta cheese.

Place the onion steaks on a dehydrator mesh with liner and sprinkle a little olive oil on top and dehydrate for 4 hours.

Add colouring (optional).

Turn the onions, sprinkle olive oil on top and continue dehydration for 8 hours or until desired consistency.

Sprouted Quinoa Salad

Ingredients

1 cup quinoa

Water to soak and rinse

The Salad

Ingredients

2 Japanese cucumbers, diced

1 red capsicum (bell pepper), diced

1 big carrot, chopped

1 cup black olives, pitted

1 bunch mint leaves, chopped

1 bunch parsley, chopped

¼ cup olive oil or sesame oil (both work well)

¼ cup lime (or apple cider or umeboshi vinegar)

2 cloves garlic, minced

½ teaspoon sea salt, more to taste (or gluten-free soy sauce)

Black pepper to taste

Honey or maple syrup if needed to taste

Method

In a large bowl, wash and rinse the quinoa well.

Soak for 24 hours and wash and rinse 3 times during this period.

To sprout the quinoa, it is best to use a sprouting jar with an attached colander.

Cover the jar with a kitchen towel.

Turn the sprouting jar upside down and place in a diagonal position.

Leave the quinoa in the jar to sprout for 1 or 2 days, remembering to rinse and drain 3 times daily.

Dice and chop the vegetables very finely.

Add all the other ingredients and mix together.

Lasts up to 5 days in the refrigerator.

A Glass Full of Goodness

Ingredients

1 apple, diced

1 stalk celery, diced

1 large carrot, grated

¼ cup raisins or any other dried fruit

½ teaspoon olive oil

¼ cup walnuts, washed

Lime & raw honey to taste

Method

Cut the apple and veggies into mouth-sized pieces.

Mix together and marinate for 2 hours or overnight.

Keep refrigerated.

Dairy Free Yogurt (CocoYo)

Ingredients

Meat of 3 coconuts (without coconut water)

½ lemon, juiced

1 tablespoon coconut oil or coconut butter

¼ cup water

Pinch vanilla pod (optional)

Method

In a fast speed blender, combine the ingredients.

Transfer into a glass jar.

Place in a dark corner and let the jar sit open and undisturbed for 12 hours to ferment.

Alternatively, use an oven with the light switched on, as an incubator.

Close the lid of the jar and chill in the refrigerator for 24 hours.

A short fermentation will result in a milder tasting yogurt.

A jar left longer to ferment up to 30 hours will taste tart and more flavourful.

Use in salads, for breakfast, ice cream, dips, soups and lassies!

Vegetable Udon Noodle Soup

The Dashi (Soup Stock)

Ingredients

4 cups water

1 big piece kombu

Lemon to taste

Miso paste to taste

The Vegetables

Ingredients

2 small zucchinis or squash

1 red capsicum (bell pepper)

2 shiitake mushrooms

Wakame (seaweed)

Spinach

Leek

Carrot

Enokitake

Umeboshi

Method

Make the dashi in a pot and let it sit overnight.

Alternatively, simmer water and the dashi ingredients for 45 minutes.

Peel and spiralise the zucchini (you may dehydrate them if you don't like them raw).

Cut or slice all the other vegetables.

Add to a serving bowl.

Charcoal (Frozen) Yogurt

Activated charcoal draws bacteria, poisons, chemicals, dirt and other micro-particles to the surface of skin, helping you to achieve a flawless complexion and fight acne.

Ayurveda uses charcoal for:

- *A bloated stomach*
- *Skin impurities*
- *Whitening teeth*
- *Facial masks*
- *Aiding hangovers*
- *Aiding upset stomachs*
- *Soothing insect bites*

Chinese traditional medicine uses charcoal for air and water purification.

Ingredients

1 cup Dairy Free Yogurt (page 217)

½–1 teaspoon activated charcoal, or more for a darker colour

Method

Add ½ teaspoon of activated charcoal to ready fermented dairy-free yoghurt.

For frozen yoghurt, add a sweetener of your choice and freeze (optional).

Tropical Sprouted Black Rice

Ingredients

1 cup black rice

1 avocado, diced

½ lime, juiced

2 oranges, diced

1 bunch basil leaves, chopped

Method

Day 1: Put the black rice into a sprouting jar. Cover with cold water. Rinse and change the water twice a day.

Day 2: Repeat.

Day 3: Repeat.

Day 4: Rinse and drain.

Combine all the ingredients in a salad bowl.

Add nuts or dried fruits of your choice.

Chatzilim Aubergine Salad or Dip

The adventure of travelling not only opened my mind in a spiritual way, it also opened my palate to new exotic dishes of foreign countries.

Everytime I make this dish, beautiful memories of the Middle East come back to me.

Ingredients

2 soft, small aubergines (eggplants)

1 tablespoon white onion, chopped

Salt and pepper to taste

1 clove garlic, minced

1/8–1/4 cup olive oil

Method

Wash and cut the aubergines into 1 cm big pieces.

In a bowl, add the aubergine, onion, garlic and marinate using just enough oil to coat well.

On a dehydrator mesh with liner, place the aubergine mixture and dehydrate at 41° C for 2–4 hours.

The Salad or Dip

Method

Make Extra Creamy Mayonnaise (page 183).

Once the aubergine has cooled down, add 2 tablespoons of mayonnaise or more to taste.

Alternatively, blend until smooth to make a creamy dip.

Kombucha

Kombucha tea originates from Northeastern China and was traditionally consumed in regions like Russia and other parts of Eastern Europe.

The key for making Kombucha tea is hygiene, sterilisation, and using wooden tools whilst your Kombucha is fermenting.

Ingredients

2 liters water

8 black tea bags

1 cup white sugar

Kombucha starter and "Scoby" (live culture with starter liquid)

Method

Boil the water for 5 minutes. Steep the tea bags in hot water for 15 minutes or longer for a stronger taste. Add the sugar.

Sterilise a wide mouth glass jar. When the mixture has cooled to room temperature, transfer to the jar. Add the Kombucha scoby and starter liquid. Using a wooden spoon, taste for the right tartness. If it's not the right level of tartness, add some white vinegar to prevent mould.

Cover with a coffee filter and rubber band or cheesecloth (breathable kitchen towel). Set in a dark corner and leave untouched for 2 weeks or longer in colder climates.

Using a wooden spoon (not a metallic spoon) return to liquid and remove the scoby and put into a sterilised container. You need the scoby to make the next batches.

Stir up the bottom of the jar and add about 1 cup of liquid to your scoby. This is your Kombucha starter and liquid for the next brew. Store in the refrigerator.

Using a funnel, bottle the Kombucha tea and store up to 1 month in the refrigerator.

Sauerkraut

I grew up in the former GDR, East Germany, behind the "Iron Curtain". I remember the joy of being able to occasionally buy bananas, tomatoes or cucumbers.

Most times the vegetable shelves of East German supermarkets were rather empty. One thing was always available: Sauerkraut.

Sauerkraut, if traditionally fermented, is a powerful food.

Probiotics like the ones in Sauerkraut improve the bacteria balance in your gut.

You can add a tablespoon of Sauerkraut or a shot of Sauerkraut juice daily to your diet.

Sauerkraut is a great source of probiotics, which provide many health benefits. It also contains enzymes that help your body absorb nutrients more easily.

Ingredients

1 kg white cabbage

15 g salt (15 g per 1 kg of cabbage)

Method

Remove the outer layer and stem from the cabbage head.

Keep the leaves aside (we use them as a cover at the end).

Using a mandoline slicer, slice the cabbage.

Transfer the cabbage into a big plastic bowl.

Sterilise a clay pot with boiling water and let it dry out.

Add the salt to the cabbage.

With your fist and fingers, squeeze and beat the cabbage until a liquid starts to form.

Fill up the clay pot to ¾ full.

Wearing rubber gloves, strongly push and press the cabbage towards the bottom.

Press until 2 cm of liquid is covering the cabbage.

Using the leftover leaves, cover the cabbage and add the fermention stone.

Cover with a lid.

Leave untouched for 3 weeks at room temperature.

Afterwards place in a cool environment for an additional 2 weeks.

Tip: *Living in an Asian climate during the rainy season, I recommend placing the Sauerkraut in the refrigerator after 3 days of fermentation.*

After 4 to 5 weeks the Sauerkraut should be ready to serve.

Bitter Melon Juice

This juice strengthens the immune system, improves respiratory health, boosts skin health and contains anti-ageing properties.

Ingredients

3 cups pineapple chunks

1 medium-sized bitter melon

Method

Remove stems from the pineapple.

Cut into chunks.

Remove seeds from the bitter melon.

Cut into chunks.

Let them sit in water with a pinch of salt for 20 minutes to remove the bitterness.

Using a slow juicer, juice the pineapple and bitter melon.

Using a strainer, remove the pulp.

Potato Chips

Ingredients

6 potatoes

¼ cup rosemary oil

½ cup apple cider vinegar

1 teaspoon kelp salt or sea salt

Method

Wash and dry the potatoes leaving the skin on.

Using a mandoline slicer, slice the potatoes into fine chips.

Soak the potatoes in cold water for about 1 hour to remove the starch.

Drain the water.

Combine all the other ingredients and marinade the potato slices for a few hours.

Drain the liquid.

Lay out the potatoes on a dehydrator mesh with liner.

Dehydrate at 41° C for 48 hours or until the desired consistency.

Bondi Beach Salad & Chili Sesame Dressing

The Vegetables

Ingredients

Green lettuces

Broccoli

Onion rings

Fresh coriander

Avocado

Cucumber

The Dressing

Ingredients

⅓ cup sesame oil

⅓ cup apple cider vinegar or lime

1 flat tablespoon Tahini

1–2 flat tablespoons cane sugar

1 tablespoon Liquid Aminos or Tamari soy sauce

3 chili, finely chopped

1 tablespoon white sesame seeds, coarsely crushed

1 teaspoon black sesame seeds, ground

Method

Using a whisk, combine all the ingredients.

Tip: *For extra flavouring add garlic, ginger or black pepper.*

Wash, dry and cut the salad leaves and cucumber.

Alternatively, steam the broccoli for 1 minute if you don't like eating it raw.

Using a mandoline slicer, slice the onion.

Shower the coriander and cut into pieces with the stems.

Put the vegetables into a salad bowl.

Using a knife, cut the avocado into halves, remove the pit and slice into thin pieces.

Using a spoon, remove from the avocado skin. Shape into a fan.

Pour as much dressing as desired over the salad.

Dressing lasts up to 2 weeks in the refrigerator.

Tip: *Top with tofu or potato chips.*

Breakfast and Dinner Smoothie

This smoothie is stable and perfect for breakfast or dinner.

The magic ingredients here are cayenne and black pepper. Black pepper reduces inflammation and is rich in vitamins and minerals.

Cayenne pepper has been used in traditional Chinese and Ayurvedic medicine to help treat circulatory problems and increase appetite.

Add hemp seeds for your daily dose of proteins. Cacao nibs are packed with antioxidants and help prevent skin damage and premature aging.

Ingredients

1 cup vegan milk and/or yogurt

1 banana

½ cup frozen or fresh mangos
(Alternatively use frozen or fresh raspberries, blueberries or mixed berries)

1 pinch cayenne pepper

1 pinch black pepper

1 tablespoon each of cacao nibs and hemp seeds

Method

In a fast speed blender, combine all the ingredients.

Add the cacao nibs and hemp seeds.

Beet Mood Salad

Ingredients

½ cup almonds

½ small beetroot (1 cup matchstick-sized)

5 shiso leaves, finely chopped

1 red apple

1 orange

1 stalk celery

⅛ cup lime juice

1 tablespoon raw honey

1 teaspoon olive oil

Method

Pour hot water over the almonds and soak for 10 minutes.

Peel the almonds.

Cut the beetroot into matchsticks and combine with the olive oil.

Cut all the other vegetables into mouth-sized pieces.

Whisk the lime juice and raw honey together.

Toss all the ingredients together.

Lasts up to 4 days in an airtight container in the refrigerator.

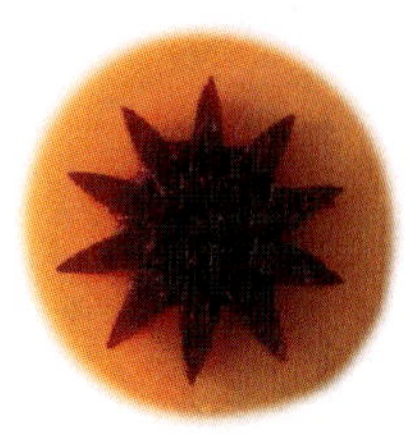

“When you swallow food that is not chewed properly, it swallows your strength, your life. Then nothing is left of you. Slow eating is one of the best meditations on this Earth”.

~ Yogi Bhajan~

Visit my website
rvz.tokyo

Find me on Instagram
zenlady_hila

Facebook
Bewilogua Hila Susanne

YouTube
Zen Lady Raw Vegan Japan